THE ART OF BEAD EMBROIDERY

JAPANESE-STYLE

MARGARET LEE

INSPIRATIONS

CONTENTS

4 Preface

5 Acknowledgements

6 **Introduction**

8 Beads

12 Equipment, Tools and Materials

22 Common Practises to Remember

24 Design Concepts

25 Finishing Process

26 **The Techniques of Japanese-style Bead Embroidery**

27 Fundamentals

28 Techniques to Create Lines

36 Surface Techniques: Single Layer

39 Filling Stitches

41 **The Projects**

46 Circles

50 Magenta Star

56 Rhythm of Beads

60 Yuletide

64 Floral Parade

72 Purple Iris

80 Hanami

84 Wedding Bells

92 Paisley Party

102 **Case Studies**

115 **General Construction**

PREFACE

For over fifty years, bead embroidery artist, Reiko Matsukawa, dedicated her career to developing and teaching Japanese-style bead embroidery. Working initially in Japan, from 1996 she taught through the Japanese Embroidery Center in Atlanta, USA, with whom I am an accredited teacher in both Japanese-style bead embroidery and traditional Japanese embroidery. Her impending retirement was recently announced and I count myself fortunate to have studied directly under her in Japan, in both a one-on-one capacity and in a group with her Japanese students. Her standards are exacting and her expectations high. When I attended my first session with her I had already completed the prescribed course in Japanese-style bead embroidery. This session was meant to round off and formalise the completion of the course I had undertaken. In her unassuming and quiet manner, she looked me in the eye and asked, "Margaret-san, are you prepared to repeat the course?" That question spoke a thousand words and thus began my true journey in Japanese-style bead embroidery. I returned to Japan over several years to study and received my Certificate of Attainment in the program from her under the auspices of Kurenai-kai, Japan. She has been an inspiration and a great role model. Her comprehensive tutelage, encouragement and enthusiasm for the art, coupled with my personal experience, inspired me to a teaching and creative role in a discipline which began as a cursory interest undertaken purely for personal enjoyment. It is now one of my great passions along with traditional Japanese embroidery and Chinese art embroidery and my aspiration is to be a conduit to pass on these three traditional art forms in their best tradition.

ACKNOWLEDGEMENTS

In every venture, there is always a group of people behind the scenes who inspire, initiate, support and make things happen. While it is never possible to acknowledge everyone, there are a few I would like to specially mention:

As ever, David, my beloved husband has been a rock with his unconditional love, support and good humour. My three daughters, Yvonne, Yvette and Yolanda and grandchildren, Aiden, Olivia and Elizabeth also continue to keep me grounded with shared love and laughter, not to mention taking the occasional mickey out of me.

Special acknowledgement goes to The Japanese Embroidery Center, Dunwoody USA for introducing this art form and traditional Japanese embroidery to the Western world. Thank you for paving the way for my personal journey in these disciplines and I honour this by carrying and passing on both the traditions of Japanese-style bead embroidery and traditional Japanese embroidery the best I can.

Professionally, in this project, I am supported by the dream team of Kristian Fleming and the editorial and production team at Inspirations Studios. It is no accident that Inspirations Studios is the premier publisher of the most beautiful needlework books and publications in the world. Thank you for making the process smooth and enjoyable.

Thank you to Kathleen Barac (stitchdolly2110@gmail.com) for her expertise in creating the diagrams and illustrations for this book and interpreting so wonderfully my poor excuse for drawing.

As ever, special thanks to dear friends Elisabeth Steimetz, Anne Ross, Carol Young and Jackie Denniston for your friendship, support, encouragement and input into this book and above all else, for being you. Special thanks also goes to Elisabeth Steimetz, Judith Truscott, Dianne Conomos and Christine Funnell for the loan of their bead embroidery as further illustration of this embroidery style.

To all those who have crossed my path and given me the privilege of introducing the art of Japanese-style bead embroidery–to you–thank you. I am sure you will see aspects of your contribution in this book.

Finally, this book is my way of honouring and paying tribute to Reiko Matsukawa. It aims to pass on the high standards and traditions that she has brought to the art of Japanese-style bead embroidery.

HAPPY BEADING TO ALL

INTRODUCTION

Japanese beadwork traces its origins to the Meiji period in Japan (1868-1912), during which western fashion inspired the application of Japanese beadwork to accessories such as handbags. These items became desirable both in Japan and Europe where fashion houses offered items enhanced by Japanese bead artisans.

Due to the long history of beads, many types of beadwork and bead embroidery are now in existence. The style of bead embroidery outlined in this book was championed by the late master Iwao Saito at Kurenai-kai, a traditional Japanese embroidery school he founded in pre-World War II Japan. Together with his handpicked embroiderer, Reiko Matsukawa, who embarked on a singular apprenticeship with Kurenai-kai, they established it as a companion art to traditional Japanese embroidery.

Although often referred to by the general term Japanese bead embroidery, this can be confusing as there are other forms of bead embroidery in Japan. To distinguish it from the other forms, I am referring to it as Japanese-style bead embroidery.

This book is first and foremost a resource for those interested in learning this technique - a unique category within the genre of bead embroidery. It is fittingly referred to as a companion art to traditional Japanese embroidery as the underlying techniques and principles originate from traditional Japanese embroidery. In place of silk threads, beads are used to create a design. Use of established techniques of Japanese embroidery, along with the non-compromising attention to detail and technical precision that is part of the practice, results in bead embroidery of superior visual aesthetics. Included in this book are practical suggestions gathered through personal experience as an enthusiastic practitioner, not only in Japanese-style bead embroidery, but also drawn from best practices in both the art of Chinese embroidery and traditional Japanese embroidery.

A teacher can learn much from her students, so over the years I have observed and listened closely to those whom I have mentored in bead embroidery and noted typical areas of concern. The answers, tips and explanations from these class interactions are also part of this book. This book is therefore as much theirs as it is mine.

BEADS IN HISTORY

Beads in various shapes, sizes and materials are known to have been used by every culture for over 40,000 years. Their role in society has been wide ranging and enduring. To mention a few better known roles, beads have been used as a medium of exchange, an indication of wealth and status, for trade, for religious rites and prayer and, most popularly, as decoration for the body in the form of jewellery and embellishment for items of apparel.

While some of these roles have become obsolete or diminished, beads for jewellery and clothing embellishment continue to be popular. Today, we refer to embellishment with beads as bead embroidery. The fact that this has endured for so long is an indication of the natural affinity that exists between textiles and beads.

The earliest types of beads were made from natural materials that could be collected or mined. These included pebbles, shells, bones, teeth, claws, seeds and natural rocks and minerals. With developments in technology, the natural path of progress, trade and the cross cultural exchanges that follow, bead variety, usage, techniques and designs expanded with time.

An important turning point for bead embroidery occurred around 3500 BC with the discovery of glass making. Glass beads were an inevitable eventuality and archaeological evidence points to the first glass beads being produced about 3500 years ago in Egypt and Mesopotamia (the present day area of parts of Iraq, Kuwait, Syria, Turkey and Iran). From this time, continuous innovations, combined with contributions from various cultures and countries as the popularity of glass beads spread, led to a wide array of bead types and finishes that are now available to a bead embroiderer.

The skills and knowledge in the making of glass beads made their way to Japan from India where a large industry was established in Arikamedu around 1000 BC. By the late 19th Century, Japanese glassmakers had learned and incorporated the process of making blown glass beads into their manufacturing and launched their own bead industry. Today, the Japanese seed bead industry is considered the benchmark for seed beads, renowned for the desirable attributes of uniform shape, size and finish. Leading the way are three well known bead manufacturers *Matsuno* (established 1935), *Miyuki* (established 1930s) and *Toho* (established 1951).

JAPANESE-STYLE BEAD EMBROIDERY

This style of embroidery is based on the concepts of traditional Japanese embroidery. Unlike other styles of bead embroidery, seed beads are used almost exclusively and traditional Japanese embroidery techniques provide the underpinning practices. Other bead types, such as crystals, are only for highlights or small feature areas rather than the main embroidery.

As with traditional Japanese embroidery, the practice of this style hinges on an understanding of the techniques employed and the visual movement and perspectives created when applied individually or in combination. Added to this, an understanding of the use of colour, the creation of different textures and a meticulous attention to detail and application in different design situations distinguishes and makes this style unique in its own right within the genre of bead embroidery.

BEADS

Beads are available to the embroiderer in diverse materials, shapes, sizes and finishes. As we primarily use seed beads in Japanese-style bead embroidery, this will be the bead type we focus our discussions on.

What then do we look for when selecting beads for embroidery?

MATERIALS

At a glance, all beads look much the same but the shine they produce is different. Beads made from synthetic materials have comparatively less shine, can suffer from wear and tear and, generally, will deteriorate over time. If made from plastic, they may also be susceptible to accidental melting when ironed.

Glass and crystal beads do not share many of the problems associated with beads made from synthetic materials. Of these, crystal beads are limited in colour and are more costly but, how they sparkle! They are useful for that special highlight that you might like to add and complement glass beads well.

That leaves glass beads, which are the bead of choice for Japanese-style bead embroidery. The range of colours available in graduated sizes and finishes leaves the embroiderer spoilt for choice. Japanese beads are available in the common sizes from 3-15, with the larger number corresponding to the smaller size for the bead. Certain finishes can be affected by sunlight and friction and these should always be highlighted by the manufacturer.

The Czech Republic produces glass seed beads which are also suitable. These beads have some characteristics which are different from Japanese beads and their selection will be based on the visual effect that one may wish to create for the project.

BEAD SIZES

Bead sizes follow standard parameters and are usually categorized as a number against /0, e.g. 11/0 refers to size 11 beads. The 0 refers to a standard bead size against which all other sizes are referenced, e.g. 11/0 refers to a bead size that is 11 times smaller than the standard 0 size. This categorization results in a bead sizing system where the larger the number, the smaller the bead.

While there are historical reasons for this categorization it is not absolutely clear cut. It has been credited to both the size of the rods used in bead making, as well as to the number of beads that make up an inch placed in a row.

Bead sizes can be confusing and often we find actual physical size differences in beads of the same referenced size between manufacturers and even from the same manufacturer. This is due to the fact that different finishes, some of which add additional coatings or layers to the bead, can change the size. As a result, size 11 beads, the most common size used in bead embroidery, can vary in size from 1.8mm-2.2mm.

The bead embroiderer should be aware of this anomaly and ensure that the actual size of the beads selected are suitable for the project in hand.

SIZE CONSISTENCY

This is a crucial factor as inconsistent sizing will distort the 'movement' that we are trying to create. If the sizes are consistent, an even effect will be created that is pleasing to the eye.

Beads from China and India tend to be less uniform than the Japanese and Czech beads. Note also that the size of the beads manufactured in different countries can vary even though they may be given the same size number. For example, for the same size reference, Japanese beads are slightly longer and have a larger hole than Czech seed beads, which are more donut shaped.

SHAPE

Seed beads are available in different shapes with more being added as manufacturers innovate in this area in response to market dictates. The most commonly used shapes are:

Round: These have nicely rounded edges and are smooth to the touch. They are the mainstay of Japanese-style bead embroidery.

Hexagon: These are faceted beads with six sides as the name suggests. The facets are even around the circumference of the bead

3–cut: These have random cuts to the surface of each bead. As a result they sparkle more as the light reflects off the surface at different levels and angles, giving each bead movement. Japanese 3-cut beads generally start with a round bead shape to which the cuts are made. Czech beads go through the same process but start out as a hexagonal bead giving a more elongated look. *Toho* 3-cut beads are sold in four sizes and use the following manufacturer's codes: size 8 – CRL, size 9 – CRM, size 12 – CR and size 15 – CRS. Czech 3-cut beads are only referenced by size and are available in size 9 and size 12.

Bugle: These are long thin tubes with flat ends and are available in lengths from 2mm–40mm. Despite the long shape, they are grouped in the seed bead category. Within bugle beads there are many variations. To name a few, bugle beads can be smooth with a round hole, twisted smooth with a square hole, hexagon bugle with a round hole, twisted hexagon bugle with a square hole. The ones that we commonly use are 2mm and 3mm smooth bugle beads with round holes.

Smooth bugle beads are used in the projects PURPLE IRIS and HANAMI in two different techniques creating totally different effects.

2–cut: These beads are similar to bugle beads. They have flat sides which give off a reflective sparkle. Sizing starts from 1.5mm.

FINISHES

Seed beads can be finished in a variety of ways, each exhibiting a different visual effect. This provides the embroiderer with a wide range of possibilities for projects. It is much like selecting threads and colours for embroidery. Finishes are usually the last part of the bead making process and some are unique to certain types of beads or to an individual manufacturer. It is therefore impossible to list all that are available in the market.

The table on the next page presents the more common coatings and finishes from the four major seed bead producers. As is the case with bead shapes and shape refinements, the coatings and finishes that are applied to beads are another area where continuous innovation comes into play.

As with any applied coatings and finishes there is the possibility of fading through long exposure to sunlight, or wear through day to day use. However this is now far more likely with cheap seed beads from India and China than with the four main seed bead manufacturers. They have all added a final firing stage into their process to ensure their coatings and finishes are as durable as they can be. As has been the case throughout history the formulas and processes used in glass production remain a closely guarded secret.

This list gives a perspective of the broad range of beads that is available to the bead embroiderer. This is both exciting and daunting especially when considering that this list is not exhaustive. In this, my advice will be to go back to the basic question – What look do I wish to create for this project? From that vantage point, choose the right beads for your project.

Stitched by Judith Truscott of South Australia

Alabaster	A dense translucent milky-white or tinted finish
Aurora Borealis or AB	An iridescent rainbow-effect finish
Ceylon	A pearl lustre surface finish or inside colouring of opalescent beads
Dyed	A seed bead that has been surface dyed to a secondary colour
Galvanised	A coloured surface coating or plating with a metal appearance
Black-lined	A black coating applied to the inside wall of a transparent or coloured seed bead adding depth of colour
Brass-lined	A brass-like coating which reflects a brass light when applied to the inside wall of a transparent or coloured seed bead
Bronze-lined	A bronze-like coating which reflects a brown light when applied to the inside wall of a transparent or coloured seed bead
Copper-lined	A copper-like coating which reflects a reddish light when applied to the inside wall of a transparent or coloured seed bead
Silver-lined	A silver-like coating which reflects light when applied to the inside wall of a transparent or coloured seed bead
Frost	Matte frosted beads typically in bronze, gold or rainbow finishes
Iris	An amazing iridescent coating when applied to dark, opaque seed beads
Lustre	A transparent bead with a subtle pearl, silver, or gold surface finish producing a soft, reflected light
Marbled	A marbled surface coating on an opaque bead. Also available as gilded marble with a further surface coating of uneven gilding over the marbled surface
Matte	Beads are etched at a microscopic level producing a matte finish that does not reflect light
Metallic	A shiny metal surface coating or plating over an opaque or transparent base giving the appearance of metal, typically bronze or gunmetal
Opal	A translucent seed bead lined with silver or gold
Opaque	Seed beads that are solid in colour
Pearl	An opaque seed bead given a pearlised surface coating
Rainbow	An iridescent coating on the outside of either an opaque or transparent bead
Satin	Seed beads made from translucent, low-lustre glass
Stripe	Seed beads made with two or more glass colours
Translucent	Glass seed beads that allow diffused light to pass through them
Transparent	Glass seed beads that are see through even when coloured. With lighter colours these beads look almost clear

Source: Courtesy of Big Bead Little Bead, an online bead shop based in the UK. www.bigbeadlittlebead.com

EQUIPMENT, TOOLS AND MATERIALS

The list of equipment and tools required is not large and once collected, these will be all that you will need for your beading projects. Having the right tools and equipment will help make the process more efficient and more pleasurable.

FABRIC SELECTION AND TRANSFERRING DESIGNS TO FABRIC

Selecting a suitable fabric for the project is a prime consideration. The stretch, weight and weave of the fabric must support the design to ensure that the shape of the project and the desired aesthetics of the bead embroidery will be preserved even with frequent use.

Fabric which has a lot of stretch is not suitable for bead embroidery. Seed beads do have a weight to them and can distort the weave of fabrics that have a lot of stretch. Suitable fabrics include quilting cotton, satin, polyester and silk with the qualities indicated. My personal preference is for either quilting cotton or silk depending on the project.

Print fabric

From time to time, we come across a patterned fabric where the design shouts out "BEAD ME". If the fabric is appropriate for bead embroidery and suitable for the project in mind, here is a ready design for embellishment. After that, it is only a matter of selecting the right beads, framing, deciding the techniques to use and starting your bead embroidery.

Transferring designs to plain fabric

Transferring a design can be done in any of the following ways:

1 **Commercial printing:** This may not be a suitable option for one-off personal use and you will need to seek out someone who offers this service.

2 **Dressmaker's carbon paper:** This comes in different colours and it is a matter of choosing one that will show on the ground fabric. Position and pin the design with the carbon face down on the fabric. With a stylus or spent ball point pen, trace the design. Ensure that tracing is done on a firm surface for best results.

Tip: It is useful to keep a spent ball point pen for this purpose.

3 **Ink jet printer:** To use a printer, first cut the fabric to paper size and stiffen it by ironing freezer paper onto the back. Feed through the printer and peel off the freezer paper.

Note: This may take some practice and you will have to ensure that the printer can take the combined thickness of the fabric and freezer paper. It does however give you neater design lines compared to the tracing method.

BEADING ON PRINTED FABRIC

FRAMES AND FRAMING UP

Any frame that supports a four way stretch will be suitable. These include stretcher bars, different variations of slate frames and traditional Japanese embroidery frames.

I would recommend that stretcher bars only be used for smaller projects as they are not conducive to making small adjustments to tension during the embroidery process should the need arise. Stretcher bars do not have the same ability to maintain tension as slate frames or the Japanese embroidery frame.

Preparing the fabric for framing:

Check that the fabric size is suitable and fits the frame that you are going to use. If you are using a slate frame with tape attached to the bars, the fabric must be a good fit.

Determine which direction of the fabric has more stretch. In most fabrics, this usually lies along the weft, or across the fabric. In framing up, the side with the least stretch should be attached along the top and bottom bars of the frame, irrespective of design orientation.

If you are using a hybrid slate frame with no tape attached or a traditional Japanese embroidery frame, you will almost always need to sew on mounting fabric to make the base fabric a suitable size. The mounting fabric should be tightly woven cotton.

1 Reinforce the side edges of the fabric. Fold under a narrow hem on each side of the fabric along the warp direction and sew approximately 2mm (1/16") in from the folded edge along the warp of the fabric on either side.

2 Cut two pieces of mounting fabric of appropriate size. This fabric should be wider than the ground fabric (in the weft direction) by at least 5mm (3/16") on each side. It should extend the fabric length by 15cm (6") on each side for the hybrid slate frames or 30cm (12") for the traditional Japanese embroidery frame.

3 Machine stitch the mounting fabric to the ground fabric reinforcing the seams at the start and finish with double stitching approximately 1cm (3/8") back.

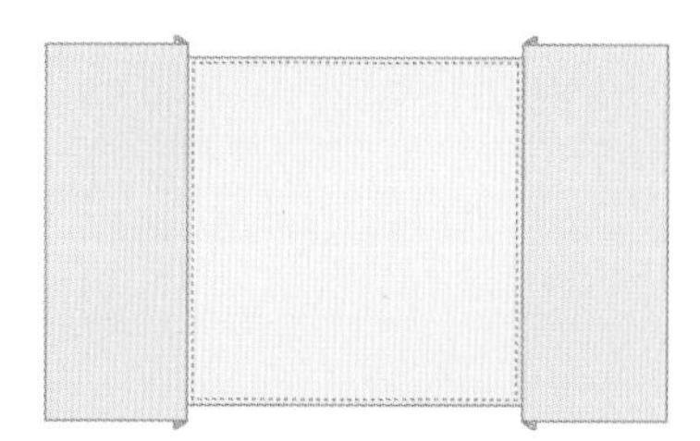

Traditional Japanese Frame

The traditional Japanese embroidery frame comprises the following components:

a) A pair of horizontal bars to be aligned to and to stretch the fabric in the warp direction.

b) A pair of weft bars to stretch the fabric in the weft direction

c) A pair of shuttle poles each of which is round and split in half lengthwise with nail holes at the end.

d) Two long shuttle nails for locking the shuttle pole in place when stretching the fabric in the warp direction.

e) Four weft pegs to lock the weft bars in position after stretching and tensioning the fabric in the weft direction.

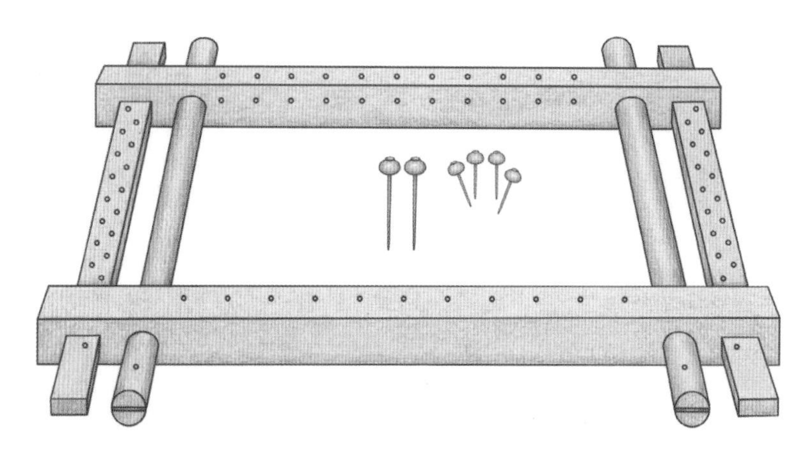

TRADITIONAL JAPANESE FRAME

FRAMING UP PROCESS

1 Insert the weft bars and one half of the shuttle pole on either side of the horizontal bars.

2 The warp of the fabric is framed up first. Drape the fabric across the frame, over the shuttle pole, lining up the warp of the fabric with the horizontal bars.

3 Insert the other half of the shuttle pole over the first half sandwiching the fabric. Leave some slack.

4 Insert the dowel nails with the point facing downward.

5 Center the fabric with some slack allowed and rotate the nail outwards from the center in a one and three-quarters rotation. At the end of this, lock the nail in place with the weft bar.

6 Repeat the for the other end. The fabric should be centred in the frame and taut on completion of step 5. If not, release the nails and make adjustments to steps 4 and 5 until the correct tension is achieved.

7 Push the horizontal bars until they abut the edge of the fabric

8 Lace the fabric to the horizontal bars, starting from the right and working towards the left.

9 Tie the lacing thread to the first hole of the horizontal bar and ensure it is secure.

10 Bring the needle down through the hole and come up in the fabric, just inside the seam allowance, a quarter of the distance between the last and next holes.

11 Bring the needle down through the fabric at the three-quarter distance between the last and next holes.

12 Bring the needle up between the fabric and the horizontal bar and repeat steps 10 and 11 until the end is reached finishing with step 11.

13 Using an awl and starting from the beginning of the thread at the right hand side, pull the lacing thread firmly. Continue for each section to remove excess thread. When the end is reached, secure the thread by looping it through the frame twice and tie off.

14 Repeat steps 9 to 13 for the remaining side.

15 Insert the weft pegs in the holes on the weft bars, on the inner side of the horizontal bars. To increase tension, pull the horizontal bars further apart and reinsert the pegs to hold to the desired tension.

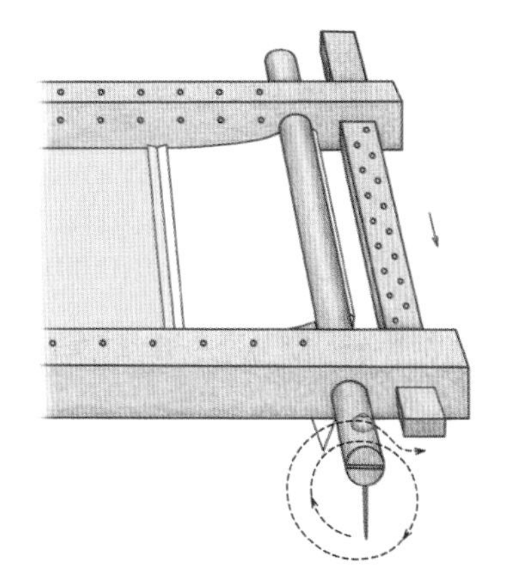

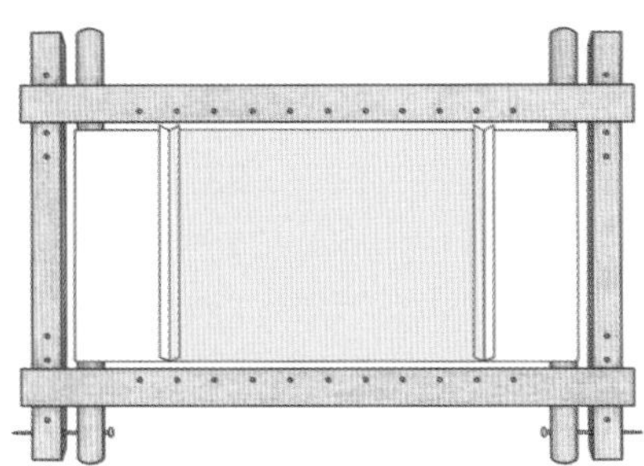

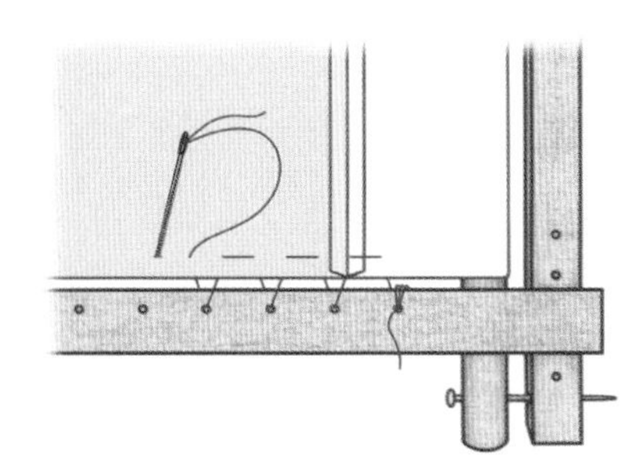

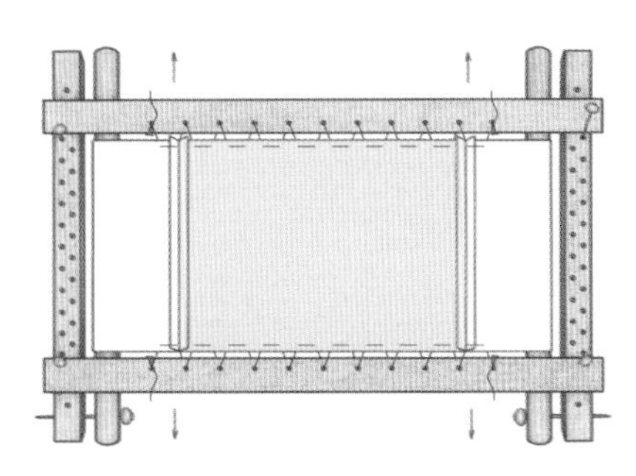

TRADITIONAL JAPANESE FRAME
FRAMING UP PROCESS

Slate Frames

There are different variations of slate frames available but they all consist of the following parts:

(a) a pair of horizontal bars with holes on each end and (b) a pair of side bars with multiple holes on each end to allow for adjustments for different fabric sizes.

FRAMING UP PROCESS

1 If the slate frame has a tape attached to the horizontal bars, centre the fabric and attach it to the tape with back stitches with a seam allowance of approximately 5mm (3/16"). Sew out from the centre to one side and then the other. Do likewise for the other end with the second horizontal bar.

2 If the horizontal bars have no tape attached, secure the fabric to the bar as per instructions for the frame. I use a hybrid slate frame which is based on the design of the traditional Chinese embroidery frame. It has no tape attached to it. Instead it has a

groove into which the fabric extension pieces are secured and held in place with a wedge strip. The cotton fabric is then rolled around the horizontal bars until the design is centred. The cotton fabric should wrap around the horizontal bars at least twice.

3 Position the weft bars into the slots of the horizontal bars. Insert the pins and adjust for tension by placing them into the appropriate holes. This step applies to both types of slate frame.

4 Turn the frame so that the side bar is positioned in a left-right direction to you. Secure the lacing thread to the horizontal bar on the right hand side and turn the thread inwards around the end of the bar to secure it.

5 Bring the needle and thread under the side bar and up through the fabric approximately 1cm (3/8") in from the edge. This first stitch should abut the horizontal bar.

6 Re-enter the fabric approximately 2cm (3/4") along to the left and 1cm (3/8") in from the edge.

7 Bring the needle up through the fabric approximately 1cm (3/8") along to the left from the last stitch and just inside the hem line.

8 Loop the needle and thread over the side bar and repeat by bringing the thread 1cm (3/8") in from the edge. Bring the needle up through the fabric approximately 5mm (3/16") along to the left of the last stitch. Repeat steps 6 to 8 until the end. Finish with step 7.

9 Do likewise for the remaining side with steps 4 to 8.

10 Adjust by pulling and tightening the lacing thread to achieve the desired tension. Secure the lacing thread by wrapping it around the frame.

Note: The lacing thread used should be sufficiently strong. Cotton thread such as DMC *broder spécial size 16 or* Presencia Algodon Tri-Finca *size 6 or 6½ are suitable.*

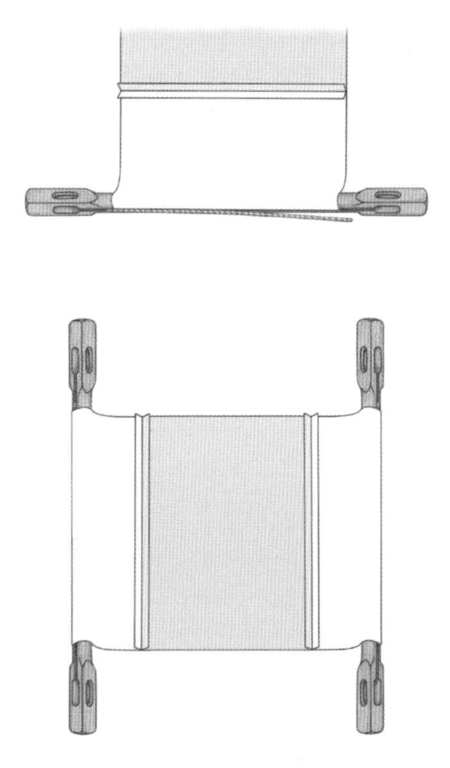

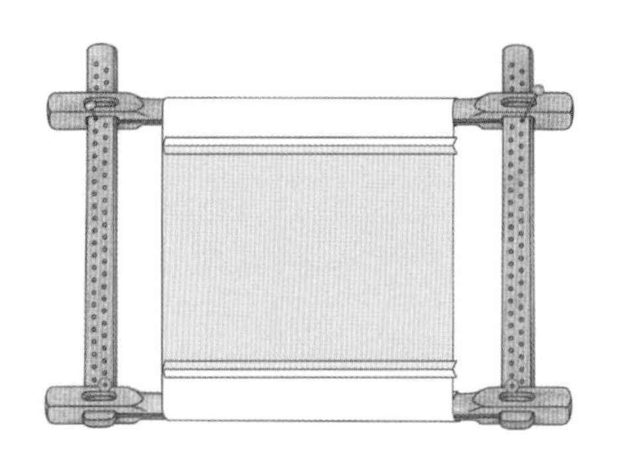

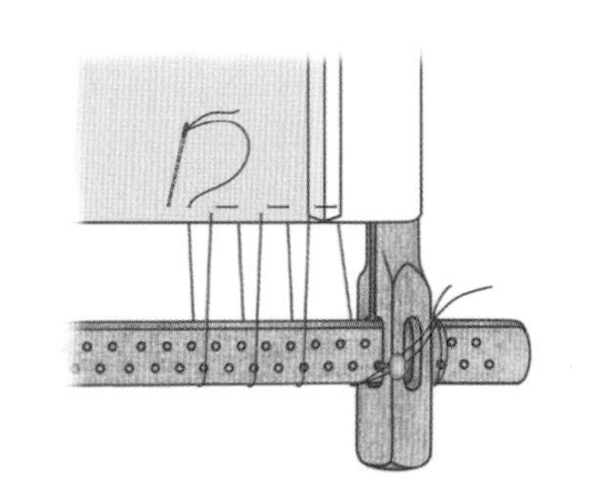

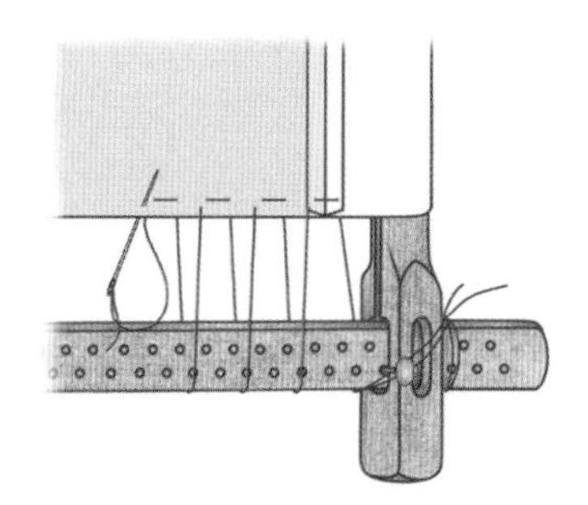

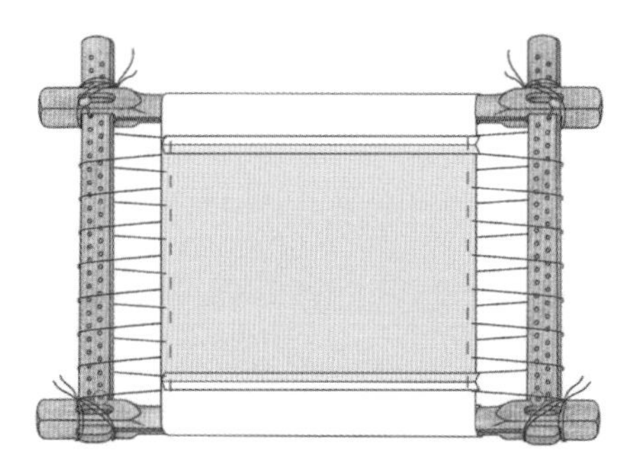

SLATE FRAME FRAMING UP PROCESS

THREADS

Cotton or silk threads can be used. As a general rule, cotton threads in either black or white in a 50 weight are used. I favour a lighter 60 thread weight which I have found to be ideal for almost all design situations. This thread is not as commonly available and the brand that I use is *Presencia.*

Polycotton threads may also be used but should be tested to ensure compatibility with the design and that lines of beads lie as they should.

White thread is nearly always used for the design embroidery and black thread is used for stitching the background if black or very dark coloured beads are used. Variations from this will be design driven.

In certain design situations coloured cotton threads or stranded embroidery floss may be used. When used with transparent beads they add a subtle colour and provide delicate colour contrast.

To provide contrast and definition, overlapping petals were worked alternately with white and red coloured threads.

Synthetic beading threads, although stronger, are not suitable as they do not always sit well on the fabric surface so I tend to avoid them.

Threads should not be waxed or treated with thread conditioners prior to embroidery as this will negatively impact the finishing process.

NEEDLES

Bead Embroidery:

The needles used should provide the practitioner with good control and be thin enough to slip through small beads without difficulty. Normal beading needles are too soft for the precise control required for Japanese-style bead embroidery.

Needles that have been tested and found suitable include:

John James Gold and Glide no.11

Clover Black Gold no.9

Clover quilting betweens no.11 and 12.

My personal favourite and preferred needles are:

Japanese embroidery M2 (for beading) and M3 (for couching). These may be more difficult to obtain as they are specialized needles.

Roxanne sharp no.12 (for beading) and sharp no.10 (for couching)

Other applications:

Needles are also required for lacing up the fabric. No.1 or 2 milliner's needles or a no.3 long darner are suitable for this job. These needles are long and easier to manoeuver for the lacing process.

SCISSORS

Embroidery Scissors

For practitioners of Japanese embroidery, Japanese made flat shear scissors which have sharp tips are used. Scissors can be very personal, so select a pair that you are comfortable with. They must be small, with a sharp fine tip to allow precise cutting close to the fabric.

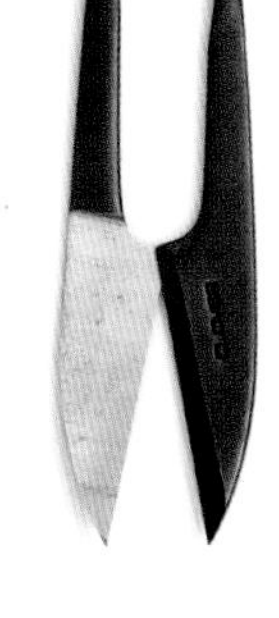

A pair of scissors for metal threads is a useful addition to the list of equipment. Metal threads work well with beads and can be incorporated into the bead embroidery.

Fabric Scissors

It is handy to have a pair of sharp fabric scissors on hand for cutting fabric. There is no specific recommendation for these and personal preference should be your guide.

Paper Scissors

A pair of scissors is also required for cutting out paper templates. It is always wise to keep separate paper and fabric scissors as cutting paper may blunt the edge of a good pair of scissors.

SEWING
TIRE
SILK

TEKOBARI OR LAYING TOOL

The tekobari is a laying tool used in traditional silk embroidery to spread, tension and lay the silk threads. This same tool is used in bead embroidery where it is used to tension and guide the threads as stitches are made. It is also used to help change the direction of beads or untwist a thread as required. In place of a tekobari, a western-style laying tool or equivalent with a tapered point can be used.

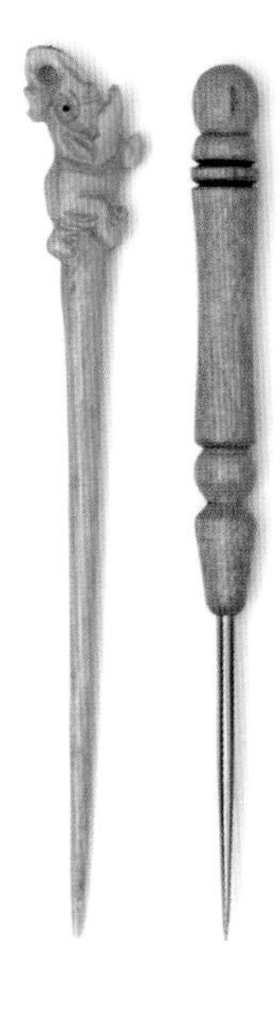

KOMAS

Komas are wooden bobbins with squared edges. They are used to help maintain tension and to position the beads that are being couched. Because of the squared edges, they will not roll on the fabric. The komas are used as a pair secured together with a rubber band or some other suitable binding. The pair sits snugly and comfortably in the palm of the hand and allows movement of the fingers. In this way, the thread can be tensioned and the fingers can assist in manipulating the beads at the same time while couching progresses.

Always ensure that the thread sits under the komas while couching as this brings the beads nearer to the surface of the fabric.

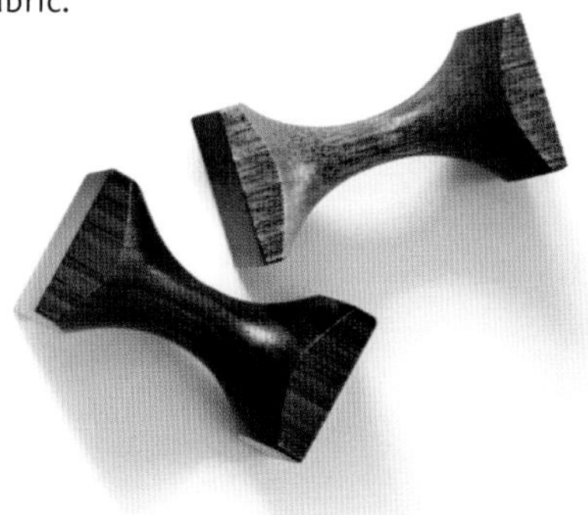

BEAD SHOE

A bead shoe is traditionally made from a piece of felt approximately 10cm (4") square. As the needle tends to catch on the felt, beading mat material is a very good alternative.

Mitre the two top corners of the square by squeezing between thumb and index finger of both hands. Bring the two mitred corners to meet at the midpoint of the top edge of the square. A bead shoe in the form of a 'shovel' is created. Stitch in place with overcast stitch to maintain the shape. These are used to contain the beads during the embroidery process and allow the beads to be brought close to the area being worked. Make up and use several bead shoes at any time. When picking up beads with the needle use a scooping motion.

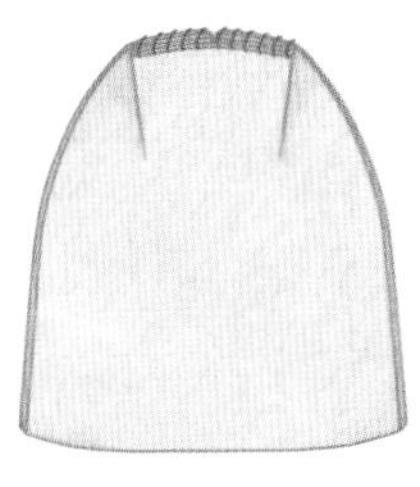

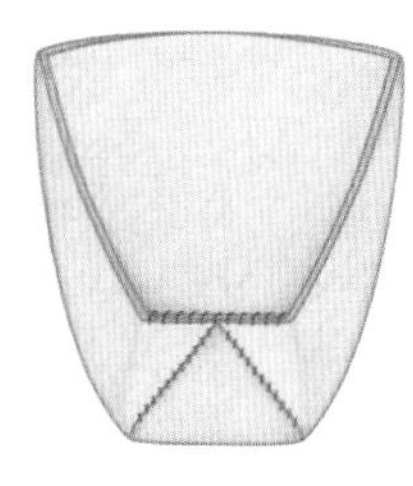

G-CLAMPS

It is usual practice to work with both hands in a coordinated manner, with the right hand on top and the left hand below the frame. G-clamps enable the frame to be held firmly to the table leaving the hands free. If a traditional embroidery frame or larger slate frame is used, the frame is first positioned between two flat surfaces such as two tables or on top of a pair of trestles and then clamped in position to prevent movement.

BEAD SCOOP

There are different models of bead scoops available. An elongated and tapered shape is preferable for bead embroidery.

PAIR OF SMALL PLIERS

These are optional but are useful for breaking beads should an odd shaped one be found. This avoids the need to remove and restring beads. An awl can also be used for this purpose but pliers are more user-friendly.

DRESSMAKING PINS

These are used for holding down the paper template or as a temporary marker when making measurements. There are different types of dressmaking pins available and glass-head pins are preferred.

DRAWING EQUIPMENT

This is optional but there may be times when you wish to re-mark a design line or make changes. I recommend a size 0.3 HB mechanical pencil or an acid-free size 0.1 pigment pen, available in different colours.

TAPE MEASURE AND RULER

For those times when you need to measure fabric, check for accurate measurements or draw in guidelines, it is useful to have these handy.

TWEEZERS

These are again optional and may be useful for removing stitches. Tweezers with a pointed tip are preferred and nothing beats a pair of *Gingher* tweezers.

DRESSMAKER'S CARBON PAPER

For tracing designs to fabric, this comes in different colours and is available in multi colour packs. The *Clover Chacopy* carbon paper is recommended. This is available in 5 sheet packs in 5 colours.

GILDING PENS

Occasionally, the design can be enhanced by adding some gilding so it is useful to have one of these.

Liquid gilt applied with a small paint brush is also appropriate.

COMMON PRACTISES TO REMEMBER

In this section common practices that apply to Japanese-style bead embroidery are introduced. These are practices that should, in time, become automatic and be applied without even thinking.

THE BEADS

Beads, like threads, can have slight colour variations between production batches. If this is a cause for concern in a design, ensure you have sufficient beads to complete the project.

Japanese beads are fairly consistent in size. From time to time, there will be a bead that is smaller than usual. Do not discard these–they are gold! Situations will arise, especially at the end of a line or in tight corners, where a full-size bead will not fit and this is the time to use them.

If you are working on a symmetrical project, divide the beads into two before commencing.

THE PIN STITCH

A pin stitch is a small stitch the size of a needle point. When properly executed this stitch cannot be felt on the face of the fabric.

Pin stitch is used every time a thread is started and ended off. To start, make a knot in the thread. Bring the needle to the front and make two pin stitches in a back stitch motion or perpendicular to each other. Ensure that these pin stitches are made in an area that will be covered by the bead embroidery. To finish off, make three pin stitches, again under a bead embroidered area. These stitches should be done as back stitches or in perpendicular positions to one another to secure the last stitch. Bring the thread to the front after the last stitch and cut close to the surface.

The pin stitch also has an important role in the embroidery process. It is used to ensure that a stitch is secured in position before moving on to the next stitch. This removes any likelihood of the stitch line moving and helps maintain the integrity of the stitches.

Pin stitch after each line of beads. The pin stitch lies along the direction of the stitch line except for any raised effect, in which case, the pin stitch will be made back under the stitch.

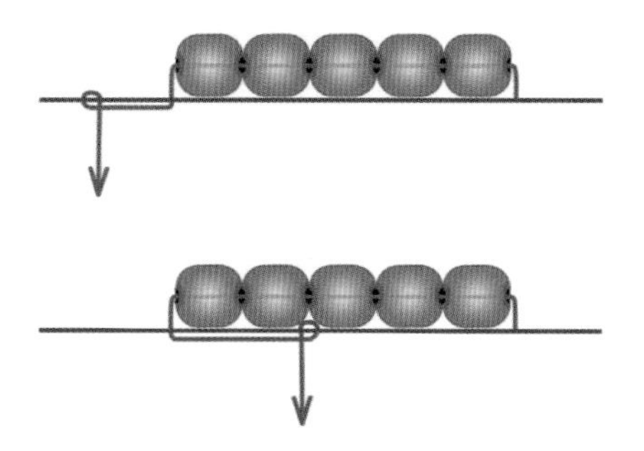

CARRYING THREADS

Threads may be carried but not more than 1cm (3/8"). For any greater distance, pin stitches at intervals of no more than 1cm (3/8") must be made. If the distance is more than 3cm (1 1/4"), it is recommended that consideration be given to finishing the thread and restarting.

THREAD THICKNESS

A double thread is used for any stitch involved in going through a bead. For couching or tying down a stitch, a single thread can be used. The double thread is achieved by threading a single thread through the needle and knotting both ends together.

SPACING FOR COUCHING

When securing a length of beads, couching will be at intervals of every bead or every two beads. Where a firmer line is required or the curve of a line is tighter, couch at every bead interval, otherwise, intervals of two beads are adequate. The first and last couching stitch must always be one bead away from the end.

PATTERN TEMPLATE

The transfer of a pattern template to the fabric is done with ***Japanese running stitch*** for curved lines or ***line of held thread*** for straight lines.

Japanese running stitch

1 Bring the needle to the front and make a stitch along the line approximately 5mm–9mm (3/16"–3/8"). The length of the stitch will depend on the curve. The tighter the curve the shorter the stitch.

2 Bring the needle to the front a pin stitch away from the end of the last stitch and repeat the two steps.

3 For best results work Japanese running stitch in a clockwise direction.

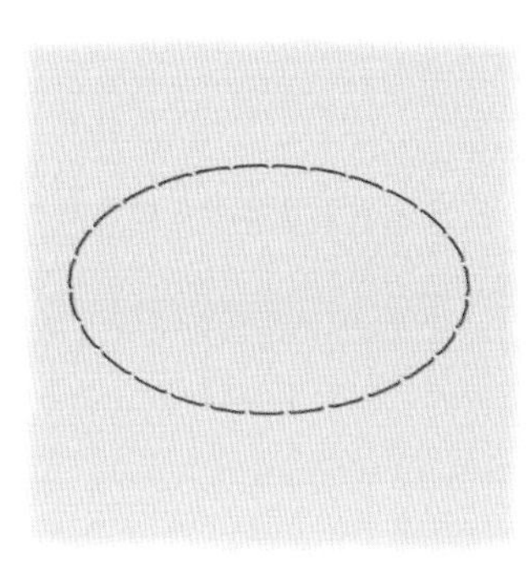

Line of held thread

1 Bring the needle to the front at one end of the line and take it to the back at the other end. This creates a plumb line, true and straight.

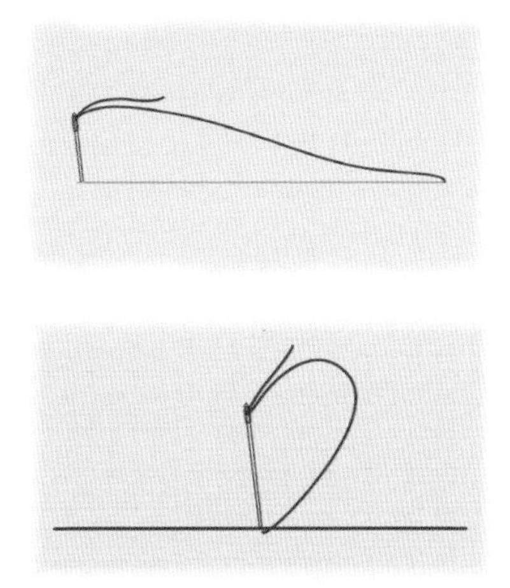

2 Tie down the stitch. The first stitch is made at the midpoint of the thread line.

3 Continue to tie down the thread at midpoints between the divided sections of the thread. Continue until the thread is fully tied along the line and the stitching interval is no less than 1cm (3/8"). Dividing and tying down the thread sequentially at the midpoints of sections ensures that the thread is secured along the line with the highest accuracy.

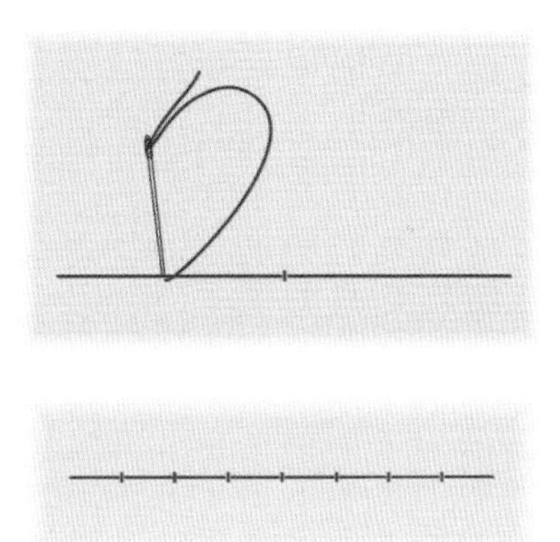

Cut out the paper template for the project and pin in position on the fabric or secure with tacking stitches. The pins should be placed in an outward direction, with at least one pin in each corner of the design. For larger patterns the tacking method should be used for greater accuracy.

Where there are corners or points in the pattern extend the two corner stitches approximately 5mm (3/16") beyond the points so that they cross each other. This will give an accurate reading to the exact position of the corner or point.

Where a pattern is made up of two sides from the same template, make a mark to indicate the position the template is facing. When marking the template for the remaining side use the same template but flip it over so that you are using the mirror image.

If an outline of beads is stitched around the design, work it outside the outlining thread. The outlining thread is taken out after the beading is complete but before assembly. It is therefore useful to use a contrasting colour thread from the ground fabric to make this easier.

MAINTAINING CORRECT SIZING

If accurate sizing is a concern, e.g. the piece is sized to fit a specific box top, conduct regular checks during the embroidery process. Everyone stitches differently and different stitch tension can result in minor changes in sizing. The embroidery should be one bead width outside the pattern template. If this is not the case, adjustments need to be made accordingly and it is better and easier to do it during the embroidery process than when the whole piece is complete.

DESIGN CONCEPTS

Techniques for Japanese-style bead embroidery are not complicated. All stitches are laid stitches according to the technique requirement and each of these techniques creates a visual 'movement'. When the techniques are applied to a design, together they create a harmonious visual movement and perspective. This is augmented by the correct selection of beads, size, shape and colour, which adds texture and further accentuates dimensional perspective.

Some concepts to bear in mind:

Bead size: Using different size beads in the same stitch will visually taper a line.

Colour: Colour changes within the same line of beads will also visually taper a line. A deeper colour is applied for this purpose. Changes in bead size and colour can be used concurrently to further enhance visual tapering.

Spacing: Increasing the space between beads at the end of a line will further enhance the tapering effect.

Negative space: When appropriately used can result in creating visual interest. It is a design concept that is all too frequently forgotten.

The one-point space: In Japanese embroidery, the one-point space is left between overlapping motifs to create dimensional perspective. This can also be used judiciously in bead embroidery for the same purpose. Leaving a gap between motifs will create the same dimensional perspective. The gap usually ranges from 0.5–1 size 15 bead space.

Density: In this respect, there should be a balance between solidly filled and lightly filled areas within the design.

Less is more: This cannot be emphasised enough. Each bead needs its own space to shine and show off its beauty. Overcrowding will not only prevent this, it will also push the beads out of their correct position and distort the lines and flow of the design.

'Feel' your design: In the process of bead embroidery let your intuition also be your guide. This is especially the case when stitching florals. When stitches are lined up too perfectly, they can look artificial and stiff. Cultivate a 'feel' for your stitches so that they flow with the overall design.

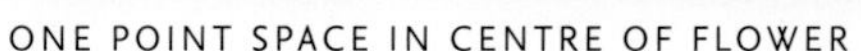

ONE POINT SPACE IN CENTRE OF FLOWER

DENSITY

FINISHING PROCESS

On completion of the bead embroidery, every piece goes through a finishing process before assembly to tidy up loose ends and, more importantly, to settle the beads and set the embroidery.

1 Do a final size check of the embroidery and check that the tension is still correct. Re-tension if necessary.

2 Check the back of the embroidery and ensure there are no stray loops or threads. If there are you need to do one of the following:

a) If the loops are short, thread up a separate needle and anchor this with two pin stitches at a distance 5mm (3/16") longer than the loop. Hook the loop with the thread and needle and pull until it lays flat against the fabric. Finish with three pin stitches and make sure these are hidden behind beads.

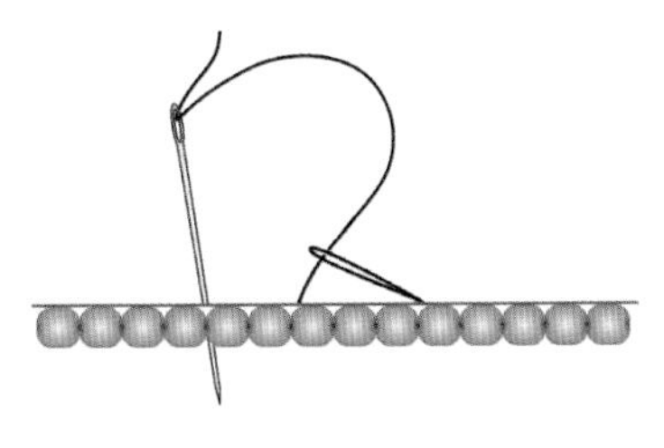

b) If the loops are long and there is sufficient length to thread through a needle, do so and secure the thread with three pin stitches behind beads.

3 With the completed embroidery still on the frame, spray with water from the back and rub on the wrong side to ensure that the water has fully penetrated all threads.

4 Place the frame with the wrong side uppermost on a sunny window sill to dry. Alternatively, place near a heater–always with the wrong side to the heat. This gentle heat and the dampening help to settle and set the fabric and threads.

5 When the piece is dry, it can be removed from the frame and constructed into the planned project.

THE TECHNIQUES OF JAPANESE-STYLE BEAD EMBROIDERY

There are three foundation principles that apply to every stitch made that will guarantee a superior outcome. These principles apply whether it is a single bead stitch, a line of beads, a couching stitch and even the pin stitch. If applied incorrectly, the design may be distorted by the stitch being out of position and/or out of line in relation to other stitches. These three fundamentals, when applied correctly, ensure a harmony and fluidity of movement to the embroidery.

Stitch Direction

The direction determines the way a stitch is pulled, which in turn determines how that stitch will sit in relation to surrounding stitches.

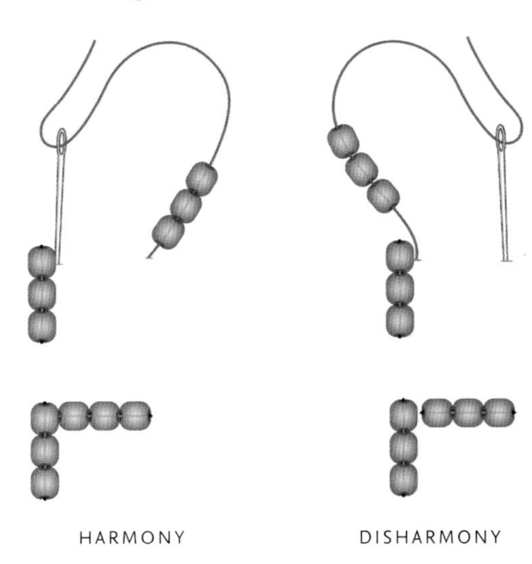

HARMONY DISHARMONY

Stitch Placement

This refers to the position where the needle comes up and goes down in the fabric. This determines the stitch line which in turn creates the visual movement of the design

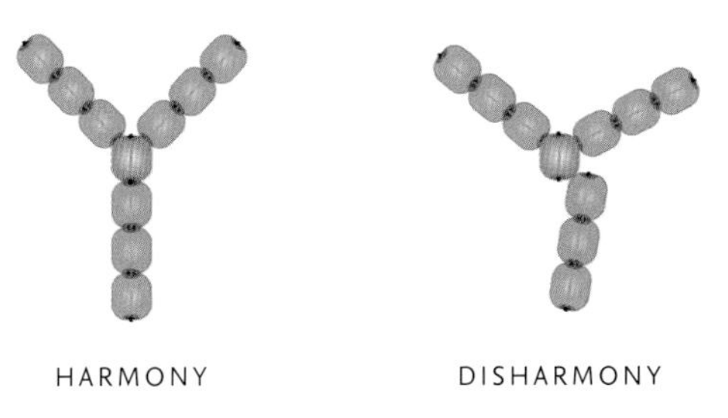

HARMONY DISHARMONY

Stitch Length

The length of each stitch must be appropriate for the number of beads. If the stitch is too short, the beads will not lie smooth and flat. If it is too long, the beads will wobble with the extra space and distort the stitch lines.

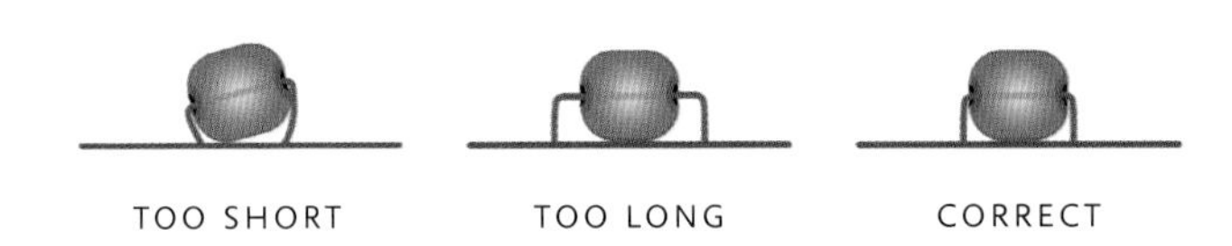

TOO SHORT TOO LONG CORRECT

TECHNIQUES TO CREATE LINES

SINGLE STITCHES

The simplest stitch in bead embroidery is that of a single stitch loaded with one or more beads. This stitch can be applied in different ways and combinations to create different effects, e.g. a simple flower is achieved by stitching carefully placed single stitches. The tutorial project, RHYTHM OF BEADS is fully embroidered using single bead stitches.

Stitches within each technique introduced are applied in a specific and prescribed method to achieve an overall effect. For each single stitch the key is to maintain correct stitch direction, stitch placement and stitch length.

single stitch one bead

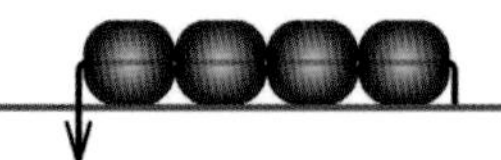

single stitch multiple bead

Line of Staggered Diagonals

This technique creates a line with a sequence of diagonal stitches of two or three beads for each stitch. These diagonal stitches introduce movement within the line and give emphasis to the curve.

To emphasise a line that curves in a clockwise direction, stitching will proceed so that the clockwise movement is maintained. Stitches are oriented in a top right to bottom left direction **relative to the contour of the curve.** This technique can be worked as a 3-step or 4-step method, with the 4-step method creating a thicker line.

3-step method (clockwise)

Begin with a single stitch that lies parallel to the curve and follow with stitches of two beads oriented in a top right to bottom left direction. Each stitch begins approximately halfway along the previous stitch.

Bring the needle up at around the midpoint of the previous stitch and make a second diagonal stitch. Some slight adjustments will be made to this position depending on the arch of the curve. Repeat this step until the end, finishing with a single bead stitch for a tapered ending. Remember to make a pin stitch after each stitch in the direction of the bead. It will help the beads to sit flat.

Beginning and ending with a single bead creates a tapered effect. If tapering is not required, omit the stitch with a single bead and begin with a stitch of two beads.

4-step method (clockwise)

Begin with a single stitch of one bead that lies parallel to the curve and follow with a second and third stitch of two and three beads respectively in a top right to bottom left direction **relative to the contour of the curve.** These second and third stitches begin approximately two-thirds up the previous stitch. Thereafter, stitches of three beads are made, all beginning approximately two-thirds up the previous stitches. Repeat this step until the end. If a tapered end is required, reduce the number of beads for the last two stitches to two beads and then one bead. Again, if tapering is not required, omit the first and last two stitches of one and two beads.

Remember to make a pin stitch after each stitch in the direction of the bead. It will help the beads sit flat.

If a slightly raised effect is desired, make the pin stitch back under the stitch itself. This should be applied only to stitches with three beads as it will not work for the one or two bead stitches.

Counter-clockwise lines

Sometimes the design line portrays a counter-clockwise movement. In this case, stitching progresses in the same manner as the clockwise curves except that the stitches lie in a top left to bottom right diagonal direction **relative to the contour of the curve.**

Alternate vertical–horizontal line

This technique creates a picot edge and is most often used for outlining small projects such as coin purses, eyeglass cases and small pouches. The outline creates a nice soft finished look for these small items.

1 Complete the outline for the pattern template. The template stitching will be the guide for applying this technique.

2 Beads are applied sequentially with pairs of beads first in the horizontal position and then the vertical position. The beads for the horizontal stitch are placed on the outside of the template pattern line and the vertical stitch is placed perpendicular to this, with one bead on either side of the template pattern line.

3 The vertical stitch can be worked in either direction but it is recommended that the horizontal stitch be worked back towards the last pair of vertical stitches. This will help to even the spacing between beads and form a smoother line. However, if a smooth outline is not required and a more random and softer effect of the picot edge is the goal, then this will not apply.

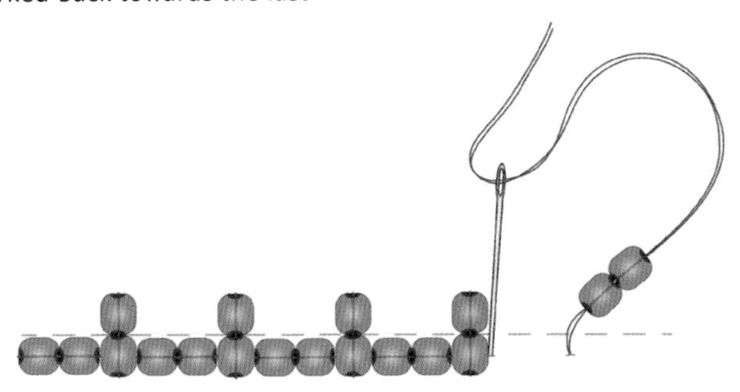

LINE OF HELD THREAD

In Japanese embroidery, this technique is used to create linear effects by holding long stitches in place along a line, often curved, with spaced stitches holding them in place. These stitches are referred to as 'tie-down' stitches to distinguish them from couching stitches that are used in relation to couching techniques.

In bead embroidery this technique is used to hold a line of beads along a design line. It is suitable for relatively shorter lines and it is recommended that the stitch lengths using this technique do not exceed 2cm (3/4") in length. A good estimation of stitch length, which should take into account the space that will be taken up by the tie-down stitches, is necessary. For a ten bead length, a good thread allowance is about the length of one and a half beads.

Line of held thread–Straight lines

1 Bring the needle to the front at one end of the line, pick up the required number of beads and re-enter the fabric at the other end. Remember to take into account the thread allowance.

2 Using the same needle and thread, tie down the stitch starting from one end. The first stitch is one bead in from the edge and thereafter is a two bead interval. The last stitch will be one bead before the end, even if it is out of line with the two bead interval.

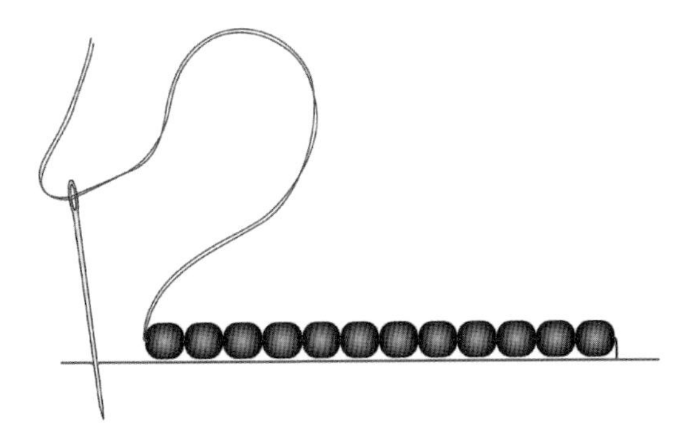

Line of held thread– Curved Lines

1 Bring the needle to the front at one end of the line, pick up the required number of beads and re-enter the fabric at the other end. Remember to take into account the thread allowance.

2 Using the same needle and thread, make the first tie-down stitch at the midpoint of the length of beads.

3 Work the first half of the divided line. The next stitch will tie down the thread at the midpoint between the stitch from step 2 and the end of the design line. Continue in a similar manner, each time tying down the thread to the design line at the midpoints of new sections created until the tie-down stitches are two beads apart.

4 Work the other half in a similar manner

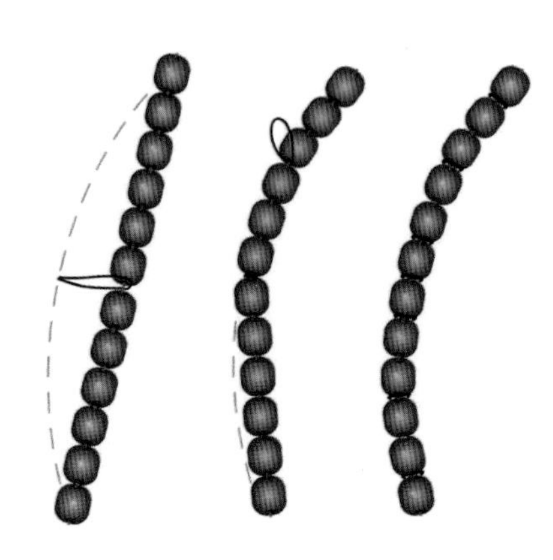

Note: If the curve of the design line is tight, the interval of tie-down stitches may need to be every bead to secure a smooth curve.

Line of Held Thread– Circle method

This method is used to create a circle of beads, usually encircling a bead or shape.

1 Bring the needle to the front at a point along the line of the circle.

2 Pick up the number of beads required to create the circle. Take the needle through the first one or two beads and re-enter the fabric along the stitch line. For small circles one bead is appropriate but for larger circles, two will provide better control. Bring the needle to the front further along the circle. Park the needle in the fabric.

3 With a second needle and single strand, tie-down between the beads beginning at the point opposite the first bead and then at midpoints between these positions. Continue tying down between each bead, shaping the circle with the tie-down stitches as necessary.

4 On completion, pick up the parked needle and give it a gentle pull to tension the circle of beads. Make a pin stitch to secure and continue the beading process.

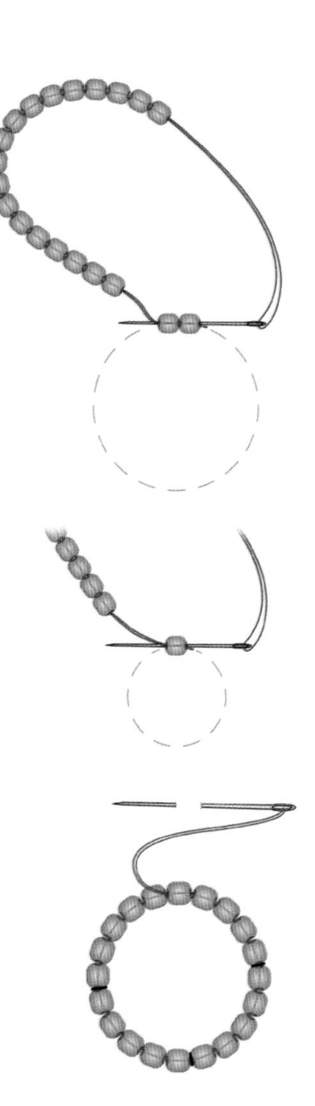

COUCHED LINES

Couching differs from the ***line of held thread method*** in that the line of beads is couched sequentially from the end with a separate needle. The needle with the line of beads is taken through the fabric only after all the couching stitches are complete. Couching is the preferred method when the lines are long or when the area to be filled is large.

General couching principles

The couching technique is worked with the aid of komas to achieve tension and help with positioning the beads to the next couching point. The mantra for couching is *'stitch... tension... position... stitch... tension... etc".* After every stitch, tension must be retained with a soft pull on the komas. Follow this by moving the komas and positioning the beads to the next couching stitch. The extra tensioning will settle the beads into position especially around curves.

Transferring beads to the komas

Before commencing, the komas need to be prepared and the beads transferred onto a double thread which will be wound around the komas.

1 The komas are used as a pair secured with a rubber band or some other suitable binding such as a length of 1cm (3/8") twill tape.

Take an appropriate length of thread, double it over and make a knot at the end. If you are working with loose beads, the thread will need to be threaded through a needle at this point before doubling and attaching to the pair of komas. As a guide, for every metre length of beads, add between 50cm–80cm (20"–32") extra to the doubled length of thread. This will provide an allowance to accommodate finishing and the couching stitches. 3m (3yd 10") is the maximum length as anything longer than that will be difficult to handle.

2 Tie the knotted end to the komas and wind the thread around the pair.

3 **Transferring beads to the threads on the komas.**

If the beads come in hanks: Japanese beads are in a standard one metre length for each hank. Attach your doubled thread to that of the hank thread and push the beads over to the doubled thread.

If the beads are loose: pour a good amount into a bead shoe and pick up in a quick scooping motion with the needle from the komas. Each scoop will generally pick up several beads and the thread will be loaded up in no time. Another way is to load the beads on with the aid of a bead spinner. The use of a bead spinner is purely optional.

Starting and ending the couching process

The following steps are standard for all couched techniques and will be referred to as 'Start the couching process' and 'End the couching process'.

1 If there is no needle attached to the komas, thread the doubled thread through a needle. For this purpose a larger needle such as a no. 9 sharp will be suitable. The eye of a beading needle is too small to thread a doubled thread through.

2 Bring the needle down through the fabric at the point where the first couched bead will sit. Make three pin stitches as if you were finishing off the stitch, bring the needle to the front and cut off the end of the thread.

3 Thread the couching needle with a single strand. Knot the thread and make the two usual starting pin stitches and commence couching.

4 Start couching at the first bead and then every two beads

5 To end, cut the thread approximately 6cm (2 3/8") from the last bead. Thread up and take the needle down through the fabric at the end of the line. Give a little tug to re-tension before finishing with three pin stitches. Finish off the couching thread similarly with three pin stitches. The last couching stitch is one bead from the end.

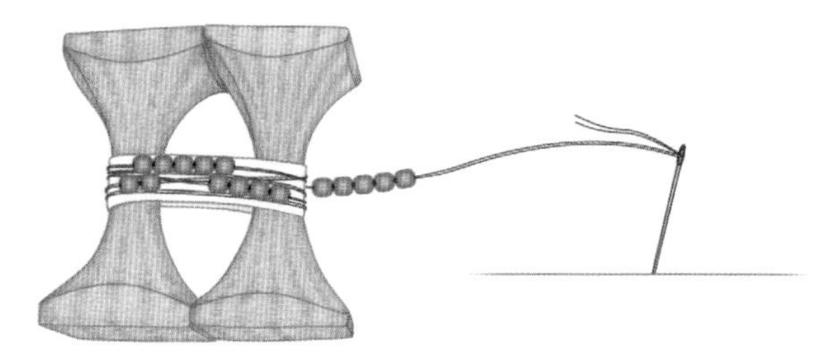

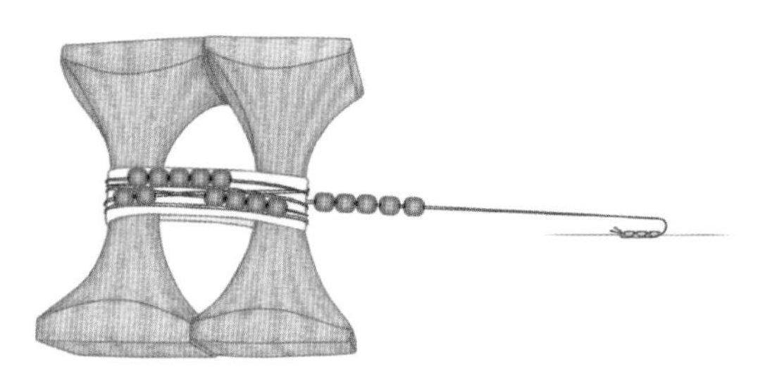

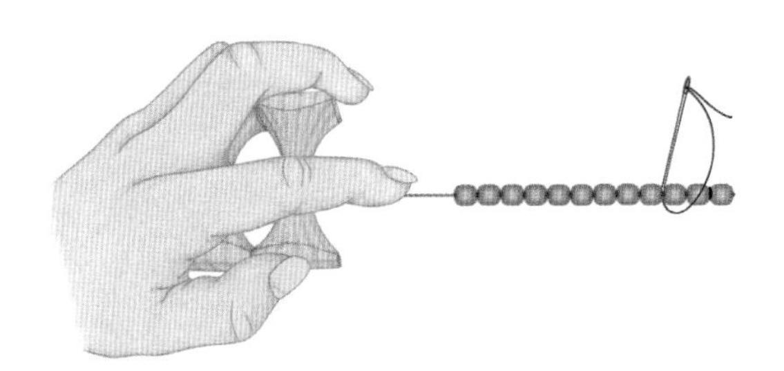

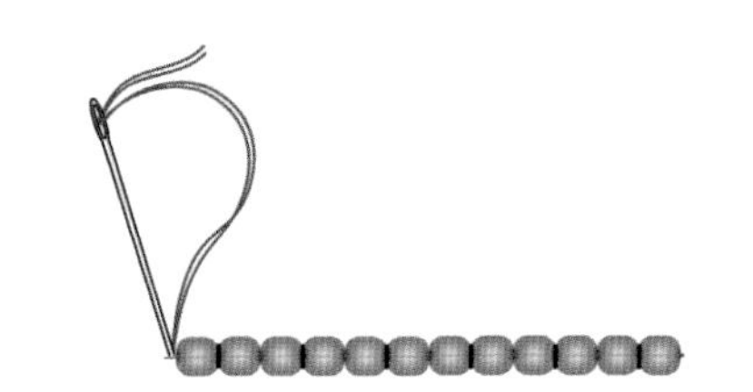

Couching Technique 1

Combination Needle-Koma Method

This technique is not a true couching technique in the pure sense but is a hybrid using the principles drawn from ***couching*** and ***line of held thread*** techniques. It is best done so that the working order proceeds in a ***clockwise direction*** and is suitable for stitching lines that are too long for the ***line of held thread*** to be effective yet not long enough for the true couching method to be applied.

1. After the usual pin stitches, bring the needle up at the starting point and pick up the estimated number of beads required for the line.
2. Wind the needle and excess thread onto the komas.
3. Starting from the first bead, couch sequentially at two bead intervals along the line. Remember the couching mantra.
4. Tension after each couching stitch by pulling on the komas.
5. With the help of the komas and keeping the thread under tension, position the beads to the next couching position and make the next couching stitch.
6. Repeat steps 4 and 5 to the end of the line finishing with the last couching stitch one bead from the end.
7. Unwind the thread from the komas, remove any excess beads and go down through the fabric at the end of the design line. Give a final tensioning tug and make a pin stitch to secure the line. The pin stitch is placed along the direction of the design line.
8. The needle and thread can travel to the next section to be stitched.

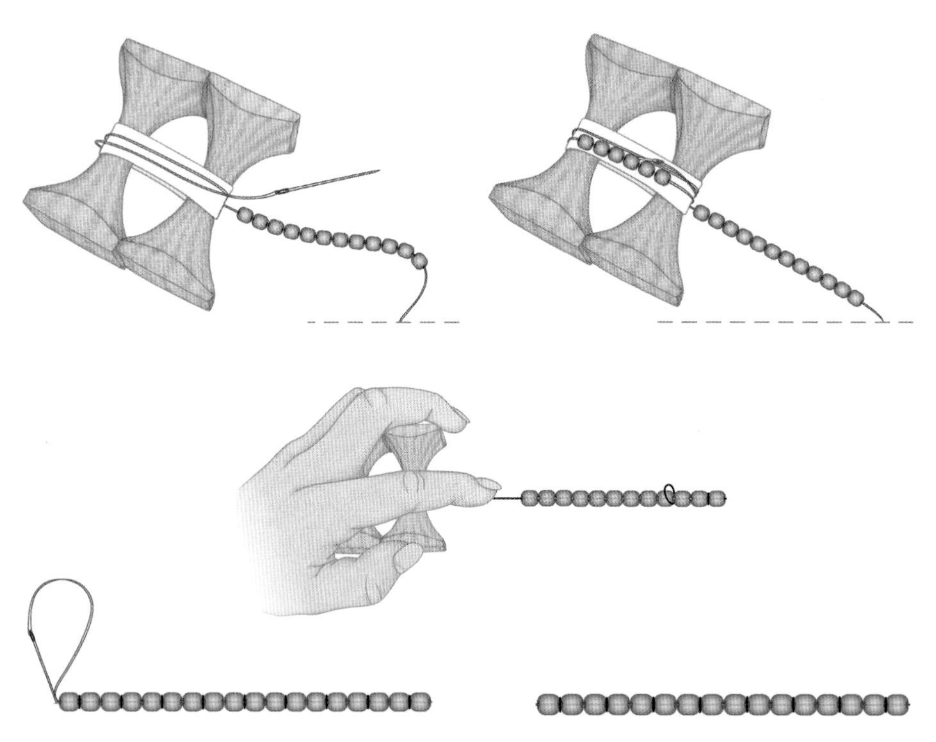

Couching Technique 2

Long Straight lines

Maintaining a straight line can be quite challenging so any help will be welcome. Here is a little technique that will assist.

1. Start the couching process.
2. After the first two couching stitches, extend the thread along the line to be stitched right up to the end.
3. Insert a pin 1cm (3/8") along the line.
4. Bring the thread around both ends of the pin in a figure eight motion. Maintain firm tension and check that the thread is exactly along the line to be stitched. Make adjustments if necessary. You now have a plumb line that is true and straight.
5. Couch the line in place as per normal with couching thread on a separate needle.
6. End the couching process.

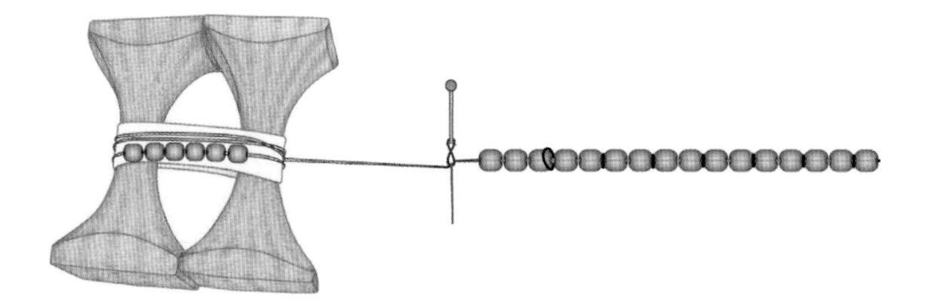

Couching Technique 3

To and Fro

In this technique lines of beads are couched beginning along one outside edge of the motif. When the end is reached, the line turns around and is couched back in the opposite direction. This process is repeated until the whole motif is covered.

This produces a visually continuous flow of uninterrupted lines. It is useful for filling regularly shaped areas. Used judiciously, it can also be employed as a means to create a regularly shaped area within another area.

Turning the corners at each end is an area that requires attention as the lines must lie true.

1 Start the couching process.

2 Approximately 7mm (5/16") from the end, make a pin stitch with the couching thread and bring the couching needle and thread to the front at the turning point. Measure out the number of beads required to complete the line and couch the koma thread.

3 The thread should be couched one point back from the perceived turning point to allow for the slight pull back when the thread is turned. Make a pin stitch with the couching thread to secure this corner stitch.

4 Go back to the line of beads and couch between each one for the last 7mm (5/16") that were left in step 2. This step ensures that the line will remain true especially at the turning edge.

5 Turn the koma thread and couch it right against the edge in a position that will start the next line of beads parallel to the first. This point will be half a bead width from the edge of the previous line of beads. Make a pin stitch to secure the couching stitch. The couching stitch that turns the koma thread should be made in the direction against the turn of the koma thread for a firm hold. When properly done, all the turning and pin stitches will not be visible.

6 Continue couching back along the line, offsetting the couching stitch for every two beads with the couching stitches of the first line.

7 Repeat steps 2–6 until the area is complete.

8 End the couching process.

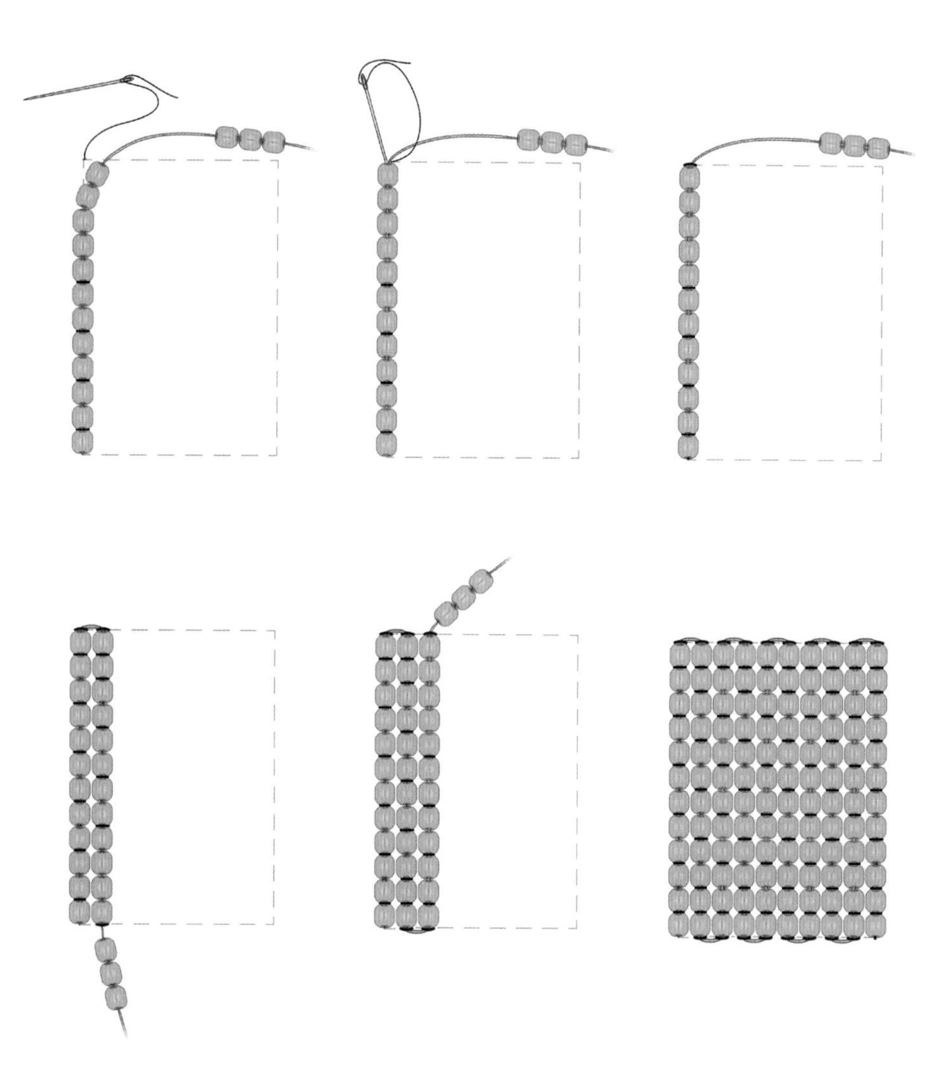

Couching Technique 4

Round and Round

This technique produces a continuous line of couching following the shape of the motif until it is solidly filled. The shape is maintained and the line movement follows around the shape. This technique will help maintain and emphasise the motif within the design.

Couching begins with the outline of the motif in a clockwise direction and continues inwards until the motif is solidly filled. The couching of each line is offset against that of the adjoining line.

For this technique, where corners exist in the design of the motif, turning these is slightly different to that for ***Couching Technique 3***.

Start the couching process at a corner and couch following the shape until the next corner is reached.

Corners can be done in one of two ways:

If the line of beads currently being couched is to form the corner stitch:

1 About 7mm (5/16") from the end stop the couching and measure and put in place the appropriate number of beads to complete the line to the corner. Make the last couching stitch for the line to secure it in place. This stitch should be as small as possible. Make a pin stitch after this stitch to secure.

2 Turn the koma thread and couch the thread right up against the edge of the last bead in a position that will begin the next line and, at the same time, form a sharp corner with the first line of beads. Pin stitch to secure this stitch.

3 Return and couch the last few beads of the first line, spacing the beads as appropriate. Pin stitch on completion.

4 Couch the first bead of the second line and proceed with normal couching principles.

5 When the motif is solidly filled, end the couching process

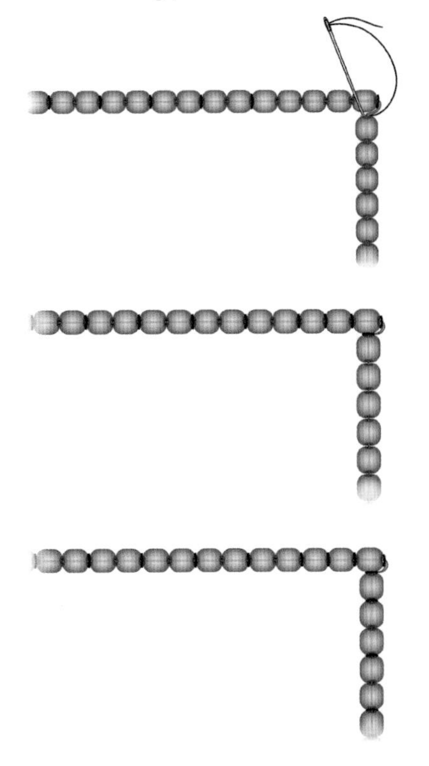

If the line currently being couched does not form the corner stitch, and the corner stitch is to be created by the second line of beads:

The last bead will stop a bead space before the corner. As with the previous method, about 7mm (5/16") from last bead, stop the couching and measure and put in place the appropriate number of beads to complete the line. Make the last couching stitch for the line. This stitch should be as small as possible. Make a pin stitch to secure this.

1 Turn the koma thread and couch it in a position that will start the next line of beads.

2 Again, check that the first bead of this line is in the right position to form a sharp corner with the beads of the first line. Pin stitch to secure this stitch.

3 Return and couch the last few beads of the first line, spacing the beads as appropriate. Pin stitch on completion.

4 Couch the first bead of the second line and proceed with normal couching principles.

5 When the motif is solidly filled, end the couching process

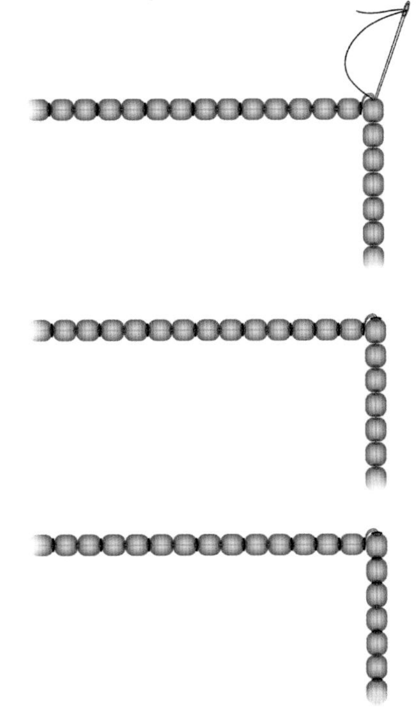

Where a corner in the motif is very sharp, it may not be possible to fill the space right at the very tip with the beads in use. In these instances, leave the space and continue to complete the overall couching. These spaces are left and filled in individually at the end with a smaller size bead.

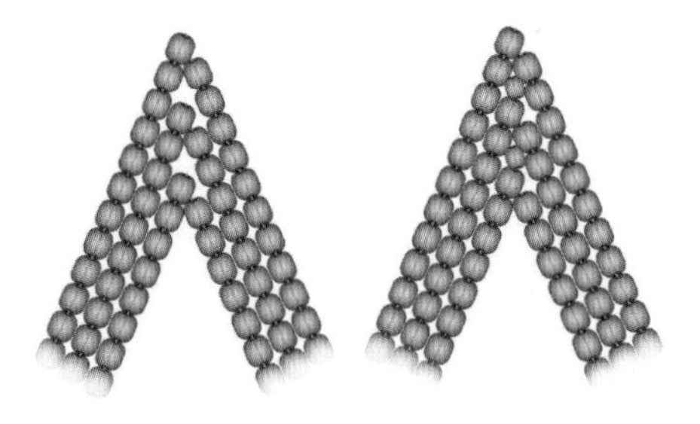

Couching Technique 5

Combined round and round with to and fro technique

In some design situations, especially over a large area the straight application of the to and fro method or the round and round method on its own may not facilitate a harmonious visual flow. This is especially the case if the motif has an outline and part of the motif is deemed to be overlapped by another motif. Two corners are therefore involved.

1 Start the couching process at one of the two identified corners

2 Proceed with the round and round couching technique until the second identified corner is reached.

3 Make a to and fro turn at this second corner and continue back with the round and round couching technique until reaching the first corner. Turn back with the to and fro technique.

4 Repeat steps 2–3 until the whole area is filled.

5 End the couching process

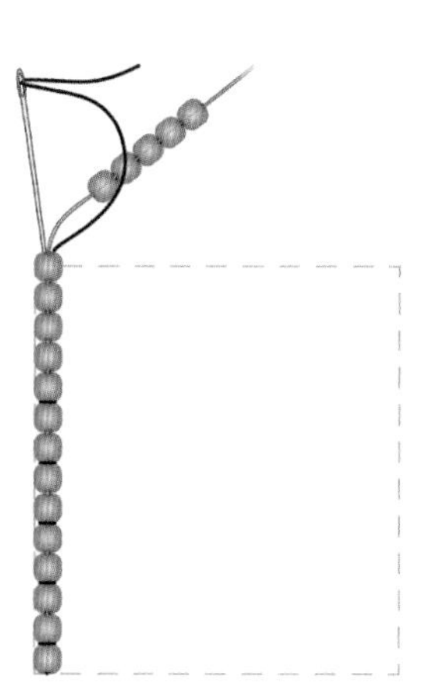

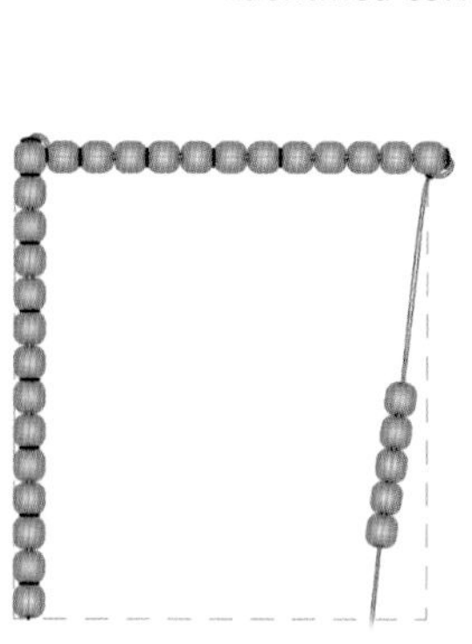

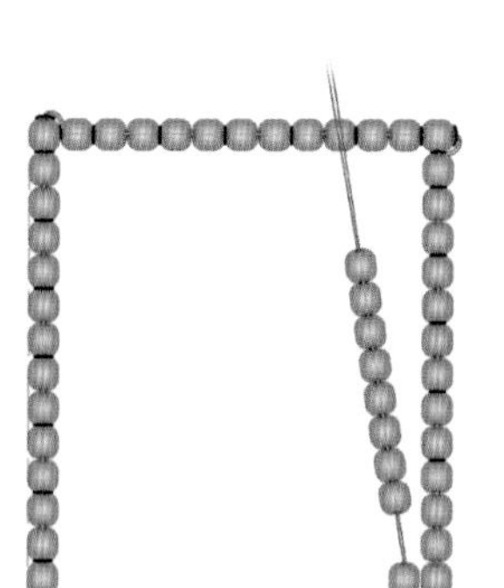

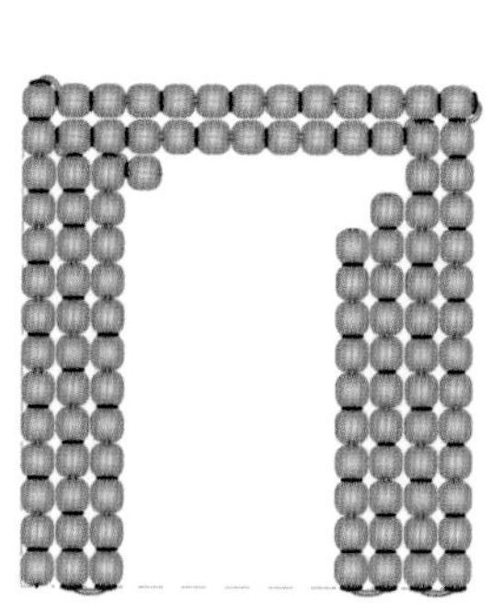

Couching Technique 6

Inward coil

This couching technique is for circular shapes. The shape is filled starting from the outline and worked inwards. To maintain a nice smooth line for the curve, couching for the first row around the outline should be between every bead.

1 Start the couching process at any point on the outline of the circle. Couching will proceed in a clockwise direction.

2 When the circle is near completion stitch to the last three beads and pin stitch the couching thread.

3 Line up the last three beads and couch the koma thread in position just past the starting stitch. This will ensure that the last bead will abut the first bead nicely and a smooth circle is achieved. Pin stitch the couching thread and return to couch the last three beads.

4 Turn the koma thread bringing it inside the circle. Couch it down inside the circle after the turn.

5 Couch down the koma thread again about two-three beads further on. Position the couching stitch so that it lines up the beads with the previous row. Proceed with couching as in the first row. The couching interval can be every two beads as the line of beads around the outline will support this second line. If the circle is small and the curves tight, it is recommended that couching at every bead interval continues.

6 Repeat steps 2–5 until the circle is filled.

7 End the couching process.

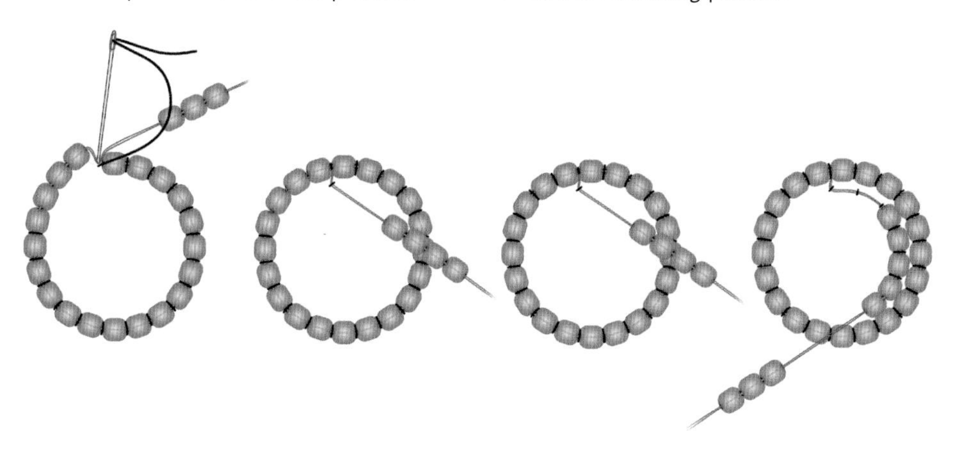

The single layer techniques are used to fill a motif from edge to edge. There are five techniques within this category and each creates a different movement and visual impression.

WEFT LAYER

- This technique will produce the least movement among the single layer techniques.
- Stitches are oriented to the weft of the fabric regardless of the orientation of the design.
- Stitches are parallel to each other.
- Commence the first stitch in a spot with a good line of reference. Work parallel stitches aligned to this stitch to complete.
- Consider using smaller beads to assist with rounded edges at both ends of the motif.

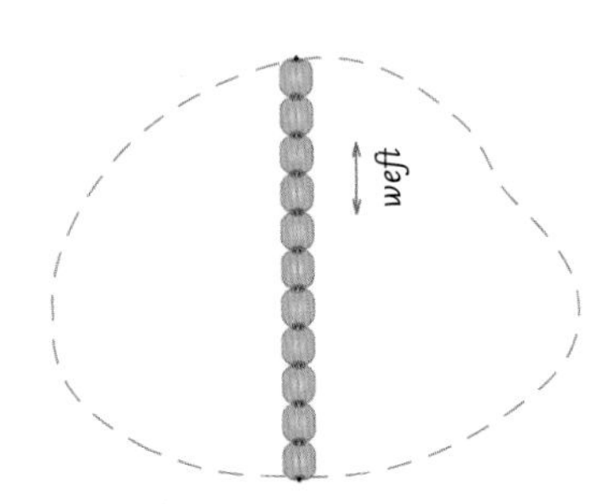

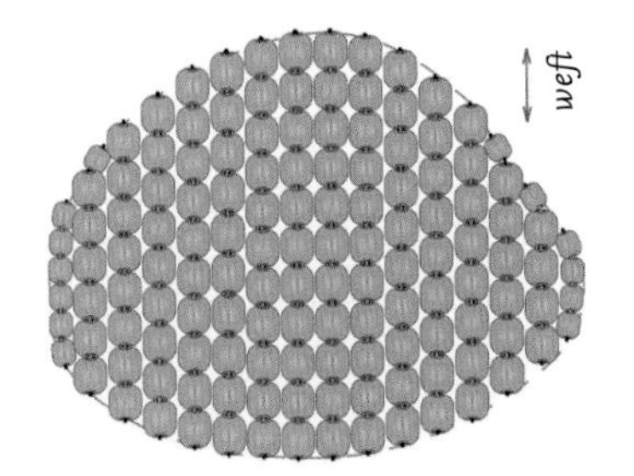

HORIZONTAL LAYER

- This is similar to the weft layer but the stitches are oriented horizontally to the motif creating slightly more movement than those for the weft layer.

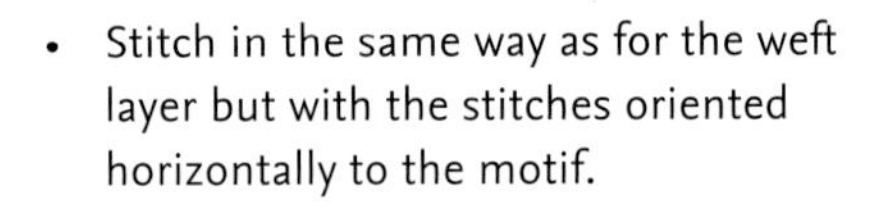

- Stitch in the same way as for the weft layer but with the stitches oriented horizontally to the motif.

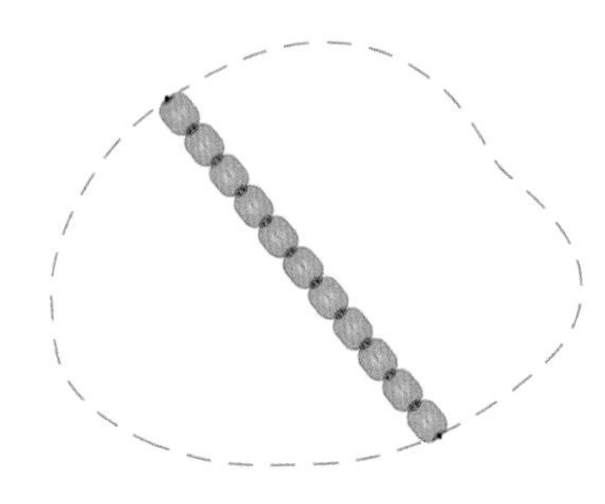

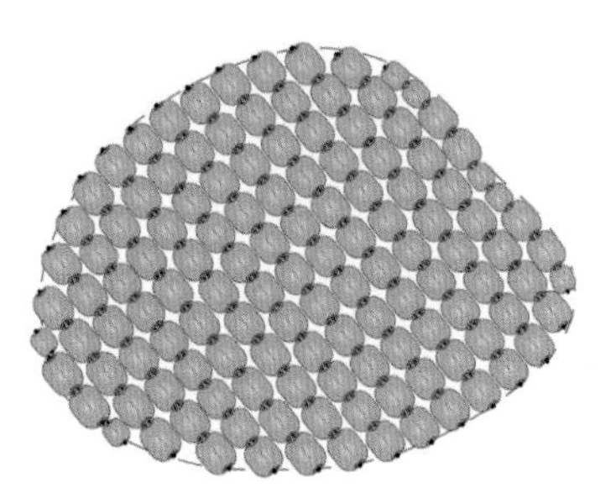

VERTICAL LAYER

Vertical layer stitches are oriented in the vertical direction of a design motif. They are more often than not used to stitch flower petals as the lines on completion simulate the opening of a flower.

- Stitch the first line of beads down the centre of the motif dividing it in half.
- One half is completed first and then the other. There are exceptions to this and these circumstances will be design driven.
- The stitches are either parallel or slightly tapered towards the base of the motif.
- Smaller beads will again assist in achieving rounded edges or tapering when applied appropriately.

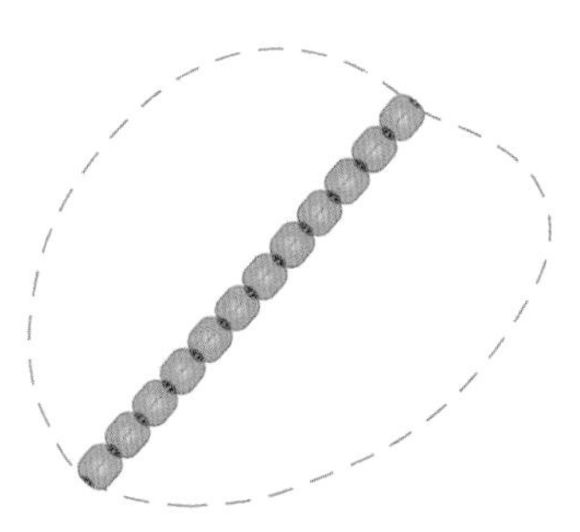

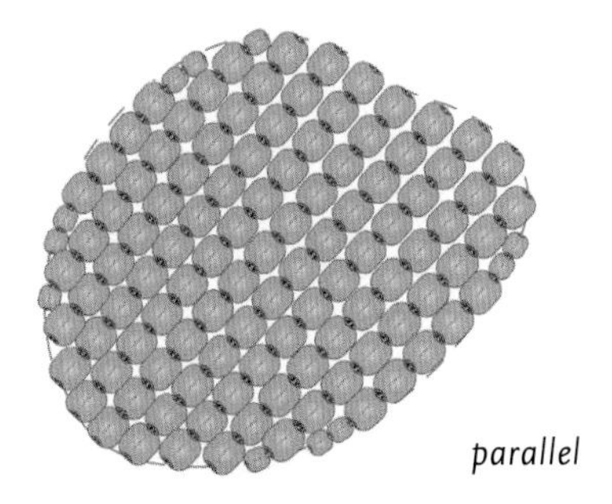

parallel

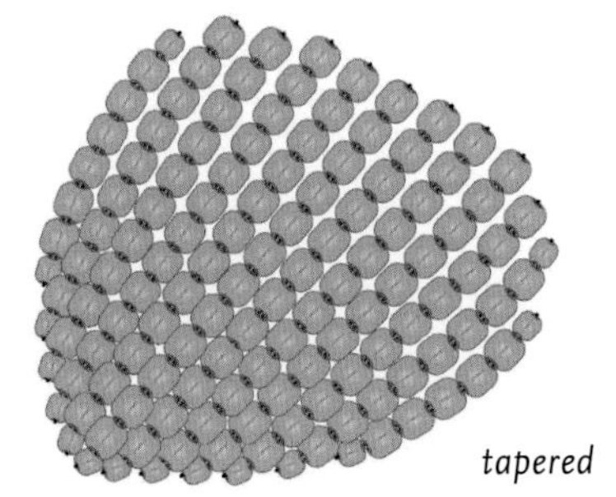

tapered

DIAGONAL LAYER

Of all the techniques, this gives the most movement to a motif from a design point of view.

- The diagonal stitches can be right or left diagonals.
- Right diagonals lie in a top right to bottom left direction **in relation to the axis of the motif being stitched**, while the left diagonals lie in a top left to bottom right direction.
- When stitching this technique, attention must be paid to the curve and the angle of the diagonal stitches are adjusted accordingly to present a fluid and harmonious movement. Generally, the angle of the diagonal stitches should be relatively steep, between 50–60 degrees, as a flatter diagonal stitch will give less movement.
- Right diagonals should be stitched in a clockwise progression and left diagonals in a counter-clockwise progression for best results.

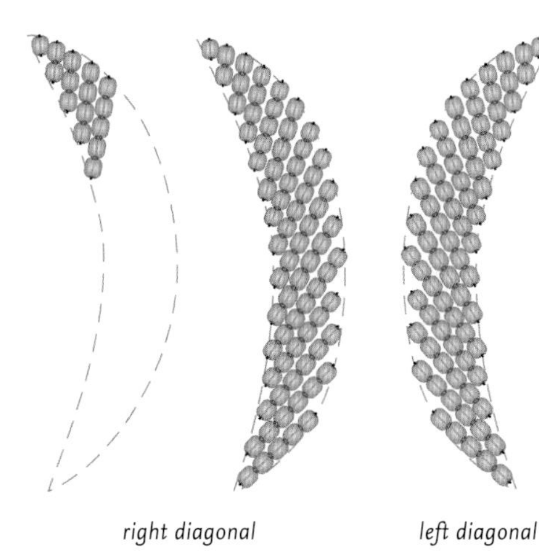

SEPARATED SINGLE LAYER

This technique is appropriate for any design motif that has a mid-line separating the left and right sides, e.g. leaves, feathers. It is based on the ***diagonal layer technique***. The right side of the two sections is stitched with right diagonal stitches and the left side with left diagonal stitches.

- The rules that apply to the ***diagonal layer technique*** also apply here.
- When stitching with this technique, the larger side of the motif, therefore being the more prominent side, is stitched first. Once completed, it provides a good visual to help ascertain the angle of the stitches for the other side to create a harmonious balance of the two sides.

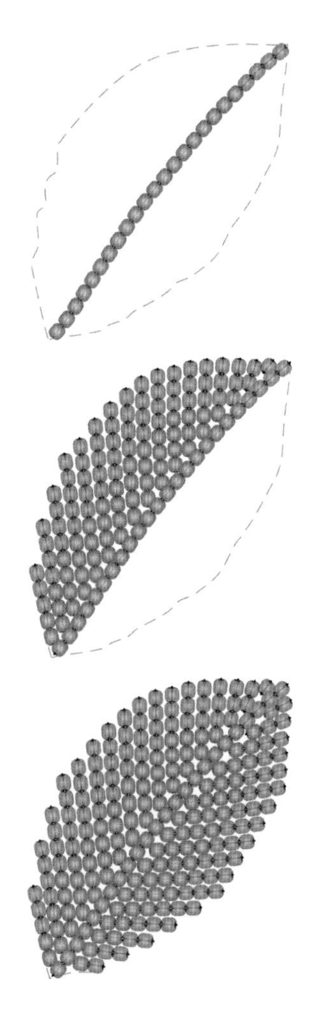

RAISED EFFECT

To give added dimension to the embroidery raised effects can be introduced. This is achieved with either one of the following:

Adjusting stitch length

This is generally used for smaller motifs, areas and shorter lines

- In this method, one, two or three additional beads are added to the stitch causing it to rise up from the fabric surface.
- There are always stitches on either side abutting the raised stitch to give it support.
- Use of colour and changes in bead sizes will help emphasise and enhance the raised effect.
- This technique can be applied with any of the ***single layer techniques*** and ***long and short techniques*** to create greater movement, texture and dimensional perspective.

Padding

This technique gives a greater raised effect with more stability. It is suitable for larger motifs with longer stitch lengths. Different effects can be created by the correct placement of padding. Beads are used for the padding.

There are two ways to apply padding:

Outline only padding

This method of padding which is only applied along the outline of a motif results in a prominent line on the outer edge. The padding line is about one size 15 bead space in from the design lines.

General padding

General padding creates a raised effect for the entire motif, not just the outline. When applying general padding, the following principles apply:

- Padding is always in the opposite direction to the ultimate surface embroidery.
- ***Line of held thread technique*** is used to apply padding.
- Padding lines begin and end one size 15 bead space in from the design line
- A tapering effect can be achieved by increasing the space between padding lines and dropping the last two stitches.

When applying surface stitching to padded areas, always stitch from the outer edge in. Surface stitching can also incorporate more than a single technique, particularly if the motif is large, to achieve the desired effect.

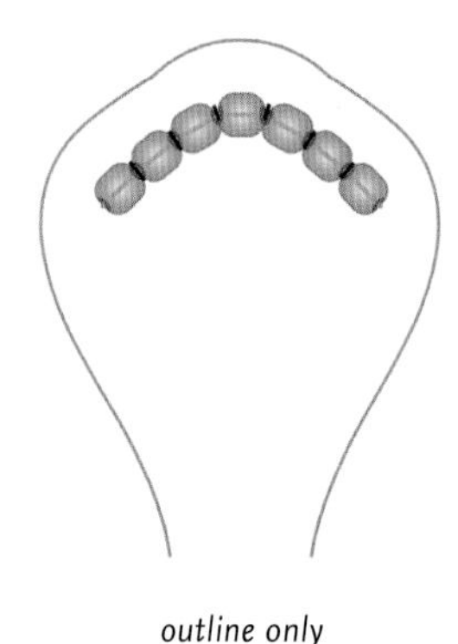

outline only

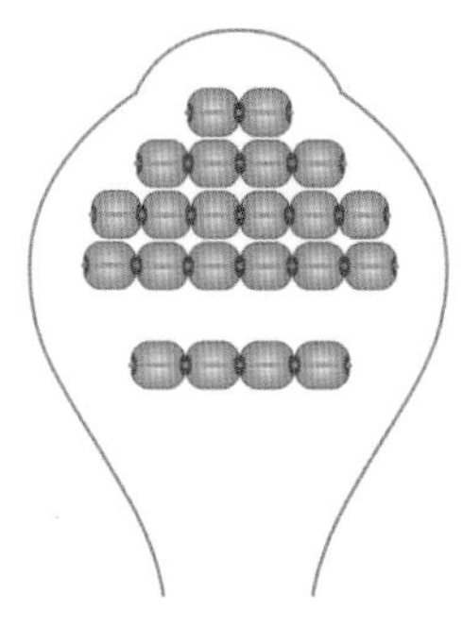

tapered

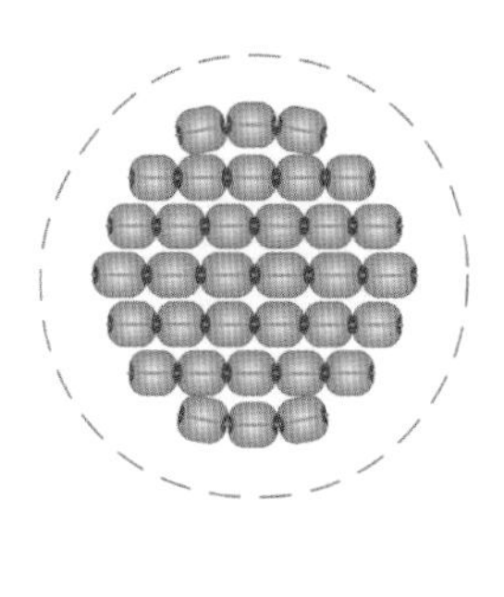

general

LONG AND SHORT STITCHES

This technique is suitable to cover larger areas and where dimensional perspective is desired.

It is often used for shapes that converge such as flower petals.

1 Determine the desired shape and its flow lines.
2 Identify the centre and commence the first stitch line at this point.
3 Work one side first with long and short stitches following the flow lines identified in step 1. When the first side is complete, work the second side in a similar manner.

Note: Padding may be added to create greater dimension. This is often in the form of outline only padding.

4 Add second and third rows as necessary, with long and short lines of beads, following the flow lines. Change the colour of beads to shade as desired.
5 As work progresses towards the centre and space diminishes, smaller beads can be used. Do not space beads too closely. Allow to fade out towards the centre.

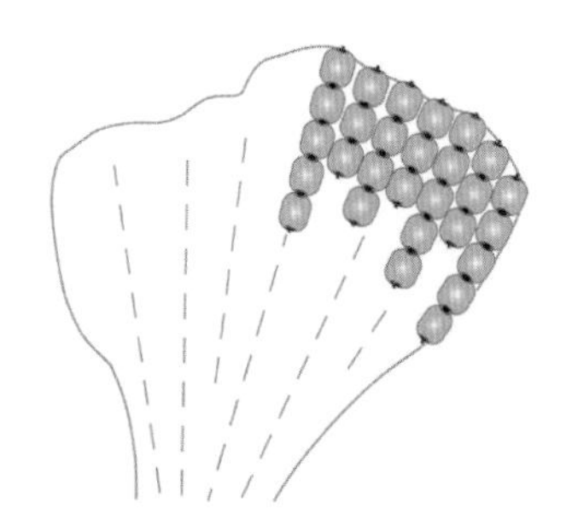

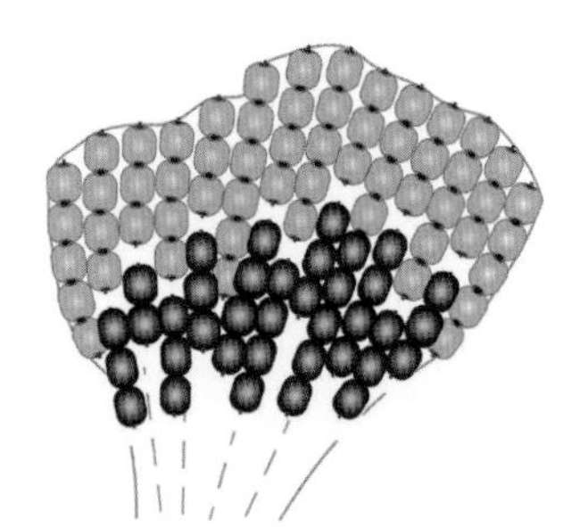

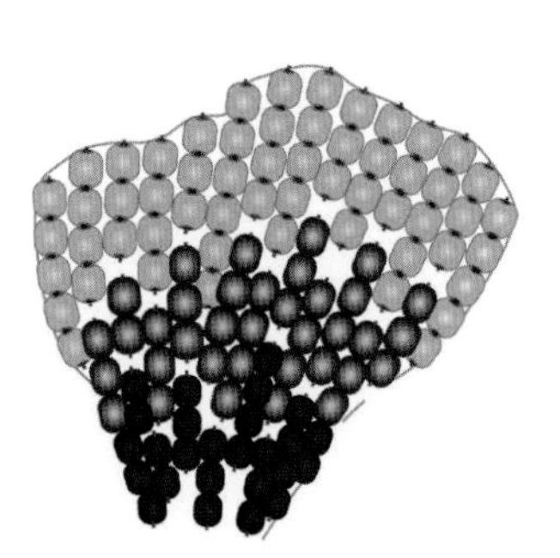

FILLING STITCHES

In this technique, the surface of a completed project or design is completely covered. Where there is background with no motif, the space is covered with filling stitches. This background space should not be confused with the negative space that was discussed in the Design Concept section.

SCATTER EFFECT TECHNIQUE 1

Spaced random placement of stitches – single or double beads

This scatter effect technique is most frequently used to fill a background to set off the motif. It provides a backdrop with a very subtle movement. Where a mottled fabric is used for the ground fabric, shadow effects are created with areas of light and dark.

In this technique single beads are applied randomly. Spacing between beads is fairly consistent and the beads are applied at random angles. It is correct that the background fabric will show through. Take care that beads do not line up or the gentle and light appearance intended will be lost.

Pin stitch after every 3–4 stitches.

Alternatively, stitches can be made with two beads which gives a slightly denser appearance.

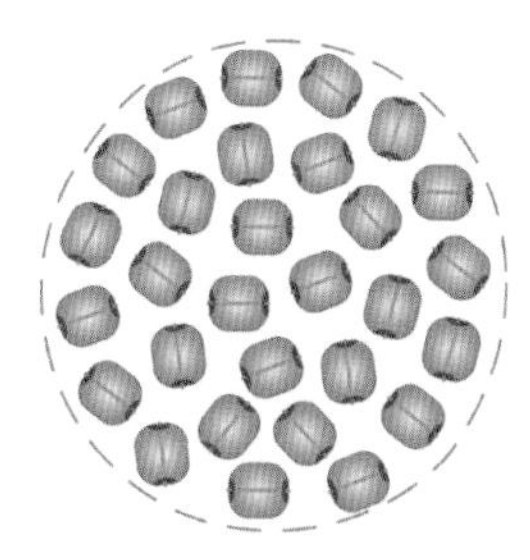

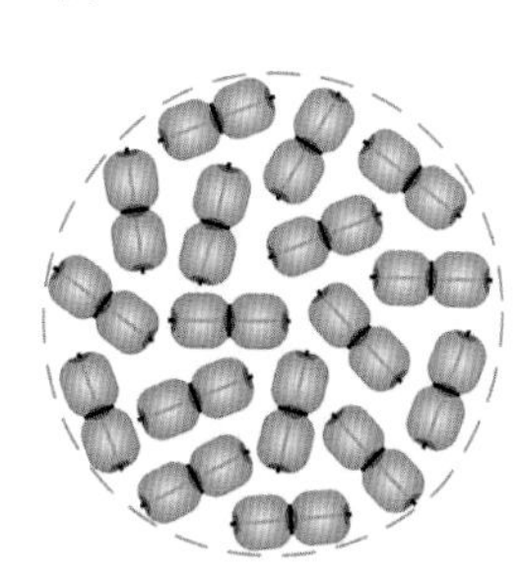

SCATTER EFFECT TECHNIQUE 2

Spaced random placement of stitches – single and double beads

This is similar to Technique 1 except that the stitches are a mix of single and double beads. The mix of beads provides greater movement to the background compared to Technique 1 which is visually more static.

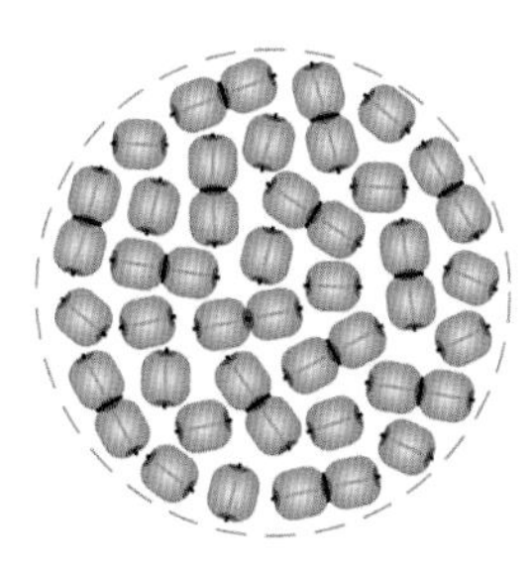

SCATTER EFFECT TECHNIQUE 3

Solid random placement of stitches

This is similar to Techniques 1 and 2 in every respect except that no spacing is left between beads. This results in a solid appearance but with an allover textured effect.

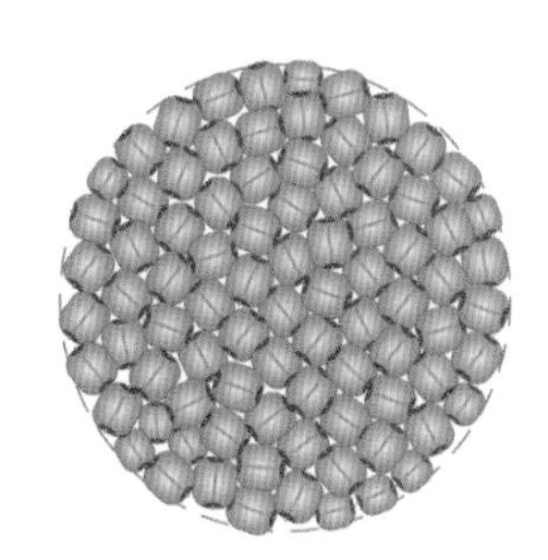

STAMEN EFFECT

This technique is used to create pollen and stamens that stand out from the centre of flowers. Each stitch represents a stamen. It is usual to make at least five or more stamens depending on the size of the flower being stitched.

1 Bring the needle to the front where you wish to position the stamen.
2 Thread between three to six beads onto the needle with the last bead in a different colour to represent the pollen.
3 Take the needle back through all the stamen beads before re-entering the fabric next to where the original stitch was brought up.
4 Repeat for the number of stamens required.
5 From a design perspective, odd numbers of stamens are preferable to even numbers.

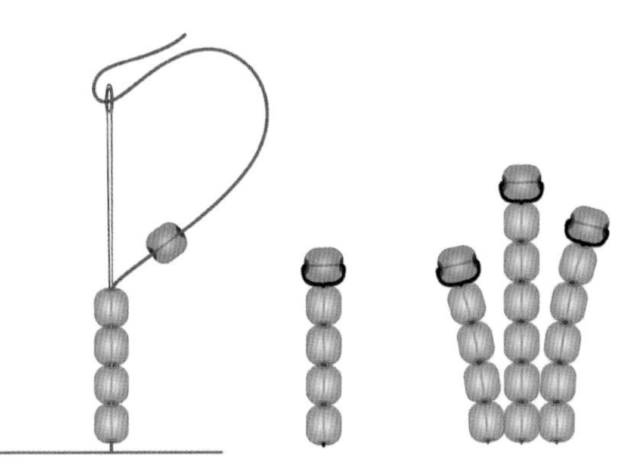

PLANNING THE STITCHING AND TECHNIQUE APPLICATION SEQUENCE

The work order in the embroidery is always as follows:

1 Outline for pattern (if called for)

2 Beading design using the following principles.

3 Background

To ensure the best possible aesthetic outcome, preserving the design lines of motifs is desirable coupled, of course, with correct choice and application of techniques. Below are some Japanese embroidery principles for guidance:

- Look initially at the overall design and identify the principal foreground motifs. Work these in order of relative prominence within the overall design. In doing so, the shapes of the design motifs will always be maintained both individually and collectively.
- When working individual motifs, identify the elements within a motif where design lines need to be preserved and work these in sequence of importance within the motif. In doing so, you will achieve maximum visual effect and retain clear design lines.
- Decide on the technique to be applied and commence stitching in the sequence as determined.

These principles and the techniques will be explored further as we apply them to the various projects in this book.

THE PROJECTS

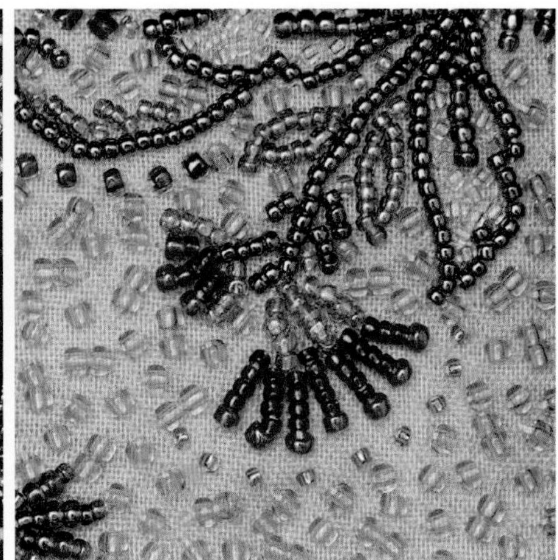

In this section, the techniques and concepts introduced earlier are translated into practice. Nine projects and two case studies have been selected to provide a diverse perspective of Japanese-style bead embroidery in practice and almost every technique mentioned in this book is covered. These projects are separated into three sections.

- **Section 1:** Three tutorial projects are introduced. They include frequently used techniques and concepts that will help to familiarize and establish groundwork.

  As a tutorial section, it is highly descriptive to assist in the transference of theory to practice and to further consolidate the knowledge base for this style of embroidery.
- **Section 2:** Six projects each of which has specific learning points and reinforces the techniques and concepts introduced and practised earlier. This section will be less descriptive and more directive. It assumes knowledge of what is covered in the first section.
- **Section 3:** Two case studies where an analytical approach from planning to completion to a given design are presented. These are aimed at consolidating all the different ideas and practices that have been presented paving the way to reinforcing the disciplined and holistic approach that is embedded in the practice of Japanese-style bead embroidery. Here are a few reminders before commencing the projects.

- Familiarise yourself with the common practices and the framing up process. These will be referred to but will not be described in detail again.
- Equipment, tools and accessories which have been listed and discussed in this book will not be repeated in the project supplies list as it is assumed that they will be at hand.
- Likewise, descriptions of stitch techniques will not be repeated but any special requirements relevant to the technique and unique for the piece will be highlighted.
- Design transfer should be made using one of the prescribed methods. Try them and use the one that is personally preferred unless the ground fabric determines otherwise. For the purpose of this book, design refers to the decorative design lines for embroidery.
- Instructions for the transfer of the pattern for the project will not be repeated unless there are prescriptive variances unique to the project. Familiarise yourself with them. Pattern in this book refers to the project templates.
- Pin stitch after each line of beads.
- The designs provided in this book are not project specific. They can be adapted and used for other projects. PAISLEY PARTY is an example of an adaptation from the one design.

TROUBLESHOOTING AND FAQS

As a general rule, this part usually comes at the end of any book or set of instructions. However, it can be helpful to know the situations that may be encountered and be able to rectify or avoid them in the first instance. The list is by no means exhaustive but represents those questions most frequently asked.

– Q –

I am not able to get a really straight line even though I am using the* line of held thread technique *when attempting to square a pattern outline.

– A –

This is not unusual if you are doing it for the first time and is probably due to one the following:

- The tie-down stitch is not in the correct position. Bring your needle up and down through the fabric vertically.
- The tie-down stitch is too long or is not perpendicular to the thread giving room for the thread to shift.

  Here is a helpful tip: *Use paper tape and place it along the line. Stitch and tie down the line using this as your guide. Remove the tape as soon as you can. It cannot be left for too long as it may mark the fabric.*

– Q –

The beads seem to flip over and I can see the holes.

– A –

This happens when the stitch length is too short for the size of the bead. Lengthen the stitch and the problem will be resolved. Note, however, that the stitch length cannot be too long or the bead may shift.

– Q –

The couched lines of beads are not sitting flat on the fabric.

– A –

This happens when beads are over-crowded or stitch tension is not correct. When couching, tension after every stitch. Remember the mantra.

– Q –

The diagonal stitches are not fitting well and I am having difficulty with stitch placement.

– A –

1. The stitching direction is incorrect. Right diagonals should be stitched travelling in a clockwise direction while left diagonals should be stitched counter-clockwise.
2. The angle of the stitches is not adjusted sufficiently with the curve of the line. In a curved shape the outer edge of the curve always has a longer distance to travel so stitches on the outer edge need to be opened up (ie more spaced) to compensate for the greater distance to be covered. The tighter the curve the more adjustment needed. Working by the guidelines set out in A1 will help with this.

– Q –

I have loaded up beads on the thread and begun couching a long line. Midway through, I find a rogue bead that is going to affect the beading. What can I do? Do I remove all the beads and take it off or shall I end off and restart?

– A –

Use a pair of small flat-nosed pliers to crush the bead. Hold a thick needle or a piece of wire through the bead while you do this.

– Q –

I have gaps between beads in adjoining stitches

– A –

This is a problem caused by any one or a combination of the following:

- Stitch direction is not correct.
- Stitch placement is not correct.
- Pin stitch is not in the correct direction.

Identify which is the one causing the problem and make the necessary adjustment to your stitches.

– Q –

I have a gap in the corners of stitches that is not covered by beads.

– A –

Try one of the following:

- Fit a bead in side on.
- Use a small bead in the same colour.
- Use a small bead in the same colour but fit it side on.

As you work, you will occasionally come across a bead that is smaller or thinner than others. These should be put aside and used when these situations arise.

If using 3-cut beads, you can generally find beads which are smaller in size due to the random cuts. Look for these beads to fit into the small space.

– Q –

I wish to define between overlapping motifs but do not wish to use negative spacing for this. Is there another way?

– A –

Using a one point gap is the most effective, but, if this is too harsh and you wish to create a more subtle distinction, use a small clear bead, usually a size 15 clear transparent for the last bead in the stitch. This is usually enough as it creates a line of muted effect between the motifs.

– Q –

My couched lines around curves are not as smooth as I wish.

– A –

The first thing that you should check is the tension of the bead thread and that the length and placement of the couching stitches are accurate. Additionally, make sure that you are working in a clockwise direction as much as possible (though not always possible when couching long wavy lines or a significant area) and make your couching stitch direction go from the inside of the curve outwards. Couching in this direction will give a firmer support for the line of beads around curves.

– Q –

I do not seem to have the same number of beads as the sample project.

– A –

We all stitch differently and this can sometimes change the number of beads required on a stitch and the number of stitches required to complete a motif.

Here are two simple examples:

- We all have a personal preference in placing our needle inside, on or outside the design line when we stitch. There is no right or wrong position but it does mean that the number of beads may need to be adjusted to fit.
- When a motif begins with the common flower centre of a single bead encircled by a ring of beads, the number of beads will vary depending how far from the centre bead the needle is positioned when the encircling line of beads is stitched. Some may require eight beads and others nine. The nine beads will have a larger circumference compared to the eight and when petals are stitched, the nine bead circle may require an additional stitch compared to the eight.

Remember, it is not the number of beads that is important. What is important is how the stitches/beads are aligned and distributed. This will be dictated by the technique. If the principles of the technique being applied are followed, all else will fall into place, irrespective of the number of beads or stitches.

Bear in mind also that bead sizes may differ between manufacturers and, even with the same manufacturer, the bead type and finish may infinitesimally change the bead size. This will also impact on the number of beads needed.

– Q –

My stitches are not evenly balanced around circles and lines.

– A –

Whenever stitches need to have some kind of balance or even distribution, whether around a circle, a shape or a line, work on the principle of breaking the space or line down into manageable sections into which stitches can be easily distributed.

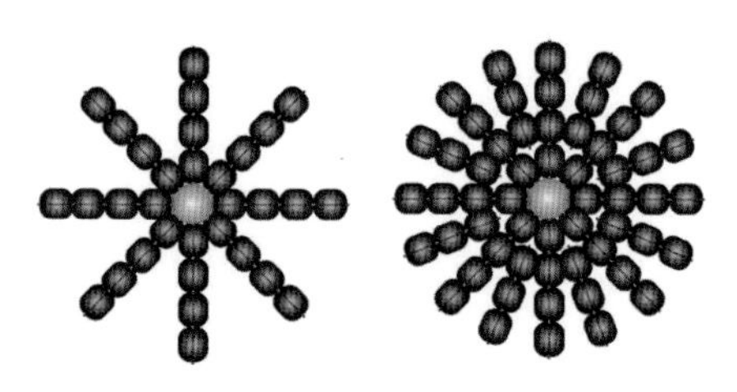

- If it is a circle, divide the circle along cardinal points and, further, along primary inter-cardinal points etc. until you obtain a comfortable and manageable section, into which stitches can be comfortably and evenly fitted.
- For a larger irregular shape, divide the space by making the first stitch down the midpoint of the shape. Work one side of the divided shape first and then the other. Consider also using a marking instrument to indicate the divisions prior to stitching. This may help to provide a visual guide for the stitches.
- For a line, apply the principle of the ***line of held thread technique*** in which stitches continuously halve the new and shorter sections of lines created until the desired space is achieved. This results in equal spacing between stitches or along a line.

– Q –

I have made a mistake with my stitch. Do I have to cut and end the thread?

– A –

It is not necessary to cut the thread. It is time for some literal reverse stitching. Hold the needle by the tip with the eye end close to the fabric. From the other side of the fabric pull on the thread until it pulls taut. Continue pulling the thread keeping it taut and simultaneously following the thread with your fingers. Keep the needle position perpendicular to the fabric and when the needle eye touches the fabric, it should follow the thread through the hole and the stitch is reversed.

– Q –

The pattern does not fit the design.

– A –

1 All fabric has some stretch, it is a matter of how much. You may have put too much tension on the fabric when framing up. Readjust. Also make sure that the warp tension is stretched first and the weft tension is stretched by the lacing.
2 Fabric stretches differently but this does not mean that you cannot use the fabric you like, so long as it is suitable for the beading. Position and adjust the pattern template to its best fit. More often than not, the variance is minor and cutting parts off the edge of the design will have no impact.

If it does, consider another fabric with less stretch or make some slight alteration to the design along the edge where it matters.

– Q –

I have a loop at the back. What should I do?

– A –

Unless this loop is the last stitch or two and can be undone easily, leave it and continue stitching. These loops will be tidied up when the beading is completed. See the section on finishing.

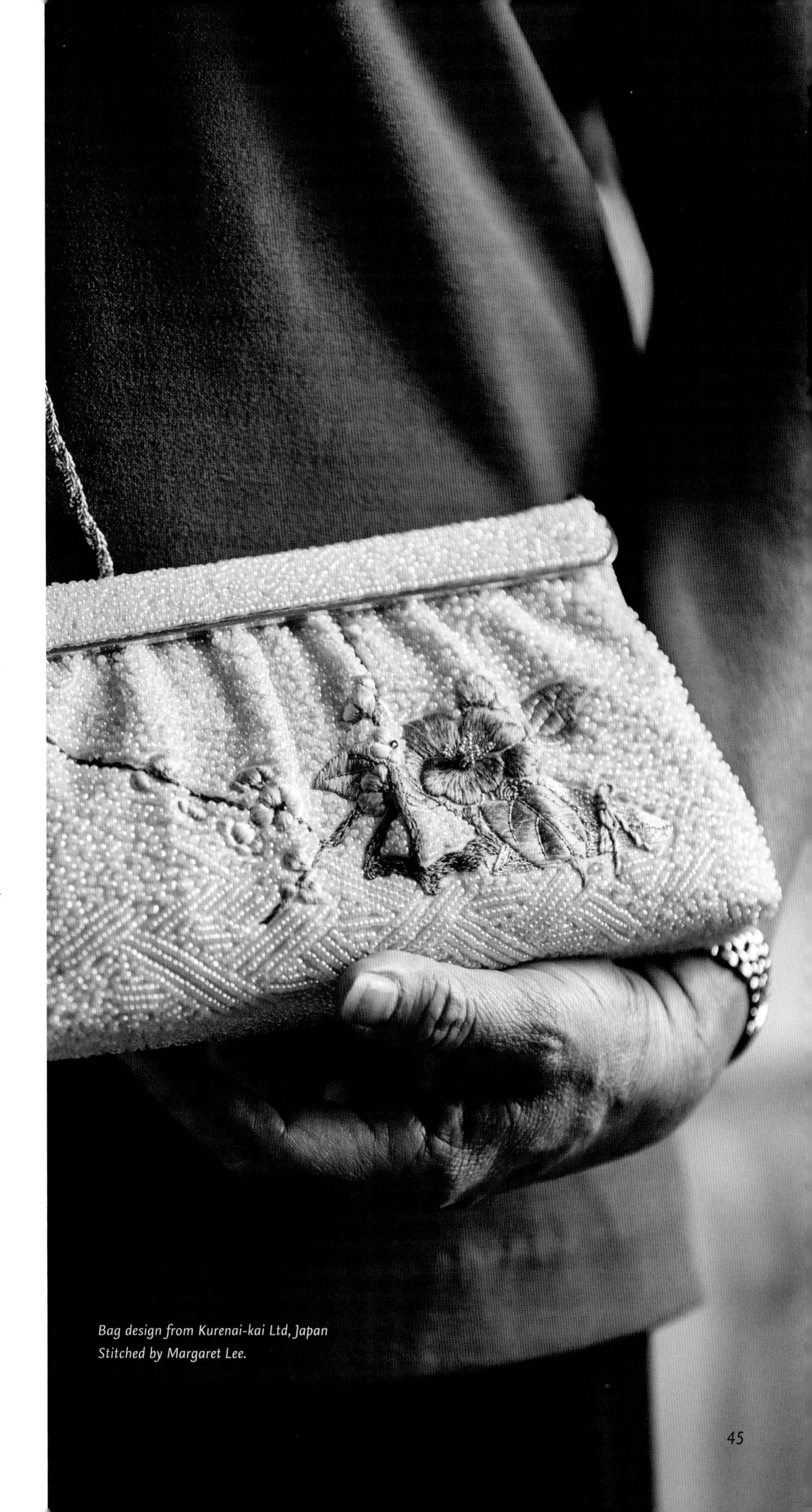

Bag design from Kurenai-kai Ltd, Japan Stitched by Margaret Lee.

CIRCLES

This is a simple design of circles but do not be deceived. This is a valuable tutorial in that it provides an understanding of and practice for the three foundation principles of stitch length, stitch placement and stitch direction. Use this project to develop an instinctive feel for these principles.

Techniques Used

Single stitches with one bead

Line of held thread

Line of held thread–circle method

Scatter effect technique 1–singles

Learning Points

The importance of the three key foundation principles will be underlined in this project
It will be immediately obvious if any of these principles are not followed

Achieving a neat circle using the ***line of held thread-circle method***

Colours and different bead types can change the look and feel of the circle motifs, particularly, the addition of the 2-cut beads to the outer circle of Circle 2

Fabric and supplies

13.5cm (5 1/2") square of cream cotton quilting fabric

8.5cm (3 3/8") square of fusible medium wadding

Square wooden box with an 8.5cm (3 3/8") square opening

Beads

Bead quantities listed refer to a 5cm x 12mm (2" x 1/2") tube

TOHO SIZE 11 SEED BEADS
A = 22 silver-lined lt gold (1/4)
B = 147 lt ivory Ceylon (1/4)
C = 177 smoky topaz rainbow (1/4)
D = 405 opaque cherry rainbow (1/4)

TOHO SIZE 15 SEED BEADS
E = 322 gold-lustre teal green (1/4)

TOHO SIZE 15 2-CUT BEADS
F = 22 silver-lined lt gold (1/4)

TOHO SIZE 12 3-CUT BEADS
G = 123 opaque-lustre lt beige (3/4)

DESIGN AND PATTERN PREPARATION

See the liftout pattern for the embroidery design.

Before any embroidery can commence the fabric must be prepared and framed up. Generally this proceeds in the following sequence:

1 Transfer the design to the fabric.

2 Frame up fabric.

3 Place pattern template over the design and outline using ***line of held thread technique.***

The sample project fits a box top of 8.5cm (3 3/8") square. Mark this out using contrasting thread and the ***line of held thread technique.*** If using a box of different size, adjust accordingly for an exact fit plus 2mm (1/16") all around.

ORDER OF WORK

The design comprises two different circle motifs in alternate sequence and rows of simple, five-petal flowers. All the larger circles are stitched first before the rows of flowers.

CIRCLE 1

1 Begin with a single bead in the centre of the circle using **B.** This stitch can be made in any direction. Work a pin stitch after the bead is applied in the same direction as the stitch.

The subsequent centre beads for all the circles as well as the five-petal flowers should be stitched in the same direction as this first bead.

2 Stitch a circle of beads around the centre bead using the ***line of held thread-circle technique*** using **E.**

3 The outer circle of beads is stitched one at a time using **A.**

a) Begin by stitching a bead at the north point followed by one to the south of the central bead. Each stitch is worked from the outer edge towards the central bead and the stitch placement is aimed at the midpoint of this bead. Stitch length must be appropriate for the size of the bead. Pin stitch in the direction of the stitch after applying the south bead.

b) Fill each half with four beads equally distributed within the space. The stitch placement is aimed at the midpoint of the central bead. Work the two halves simultaneously so that the opposite stitches line up.

c) The pin stitch is made after each second stitch in the direction of the stitch. In this way all beads will pull inwards towards the centre.

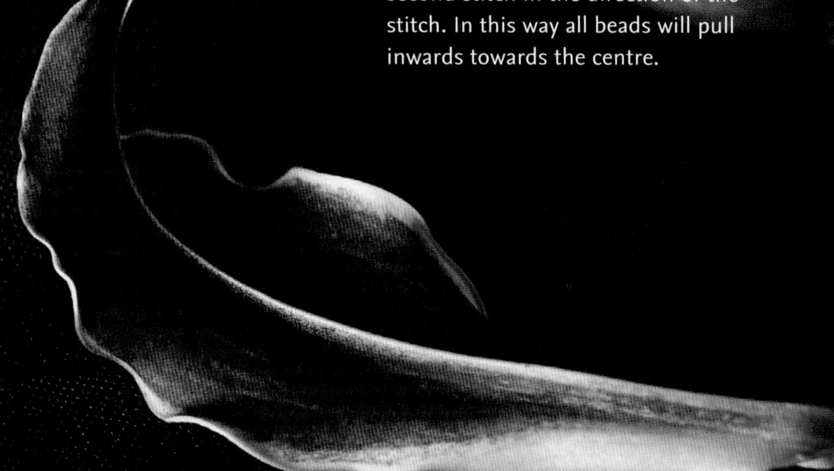

This sequence of stitches will result in a simple ten-petal flower with an even distribution of beads that flow within the circle.

CIRCLE 2

1 Begin with the centre bead in the same manner as **Circle Bead 1** using **B**.

2 Stitch the five petals of the flower, using **C** and beginning with three single bead stitches in the form a 'Y' around the centre. Each stitch is worked from the outer edge towards the central bead and the stitch placement is aimed towards the midpoint of the central bead. Pin stitch along the line of stitch direction.

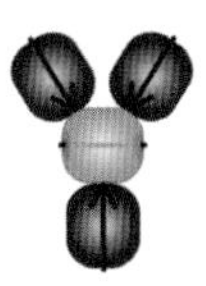

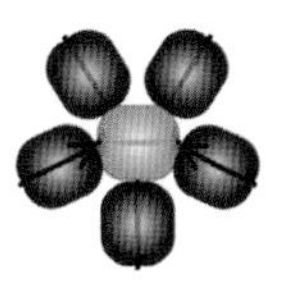

3 The third outer circle of beads is stitched one at a time using **F**.

a) Begin with a bead in the north followed by one to the south of the central bead. Each stitch is worked from the outer edge in towards the central bead and the stitch placement is aimed at the midpoint of the central bead. Stitch length must be appropriate for the size of the bead. Pin stitch in the direction of the stitch after the bead in the south. Add beads at the west and east points in the same manner.

b) There are now four equal quarters. Each quarter will be filled with two single bead stitches. Work opposite quarters simultaneously so that the opposite stitches line up. The pin stitch is made after each second stitch in the direction of the stitch. In this way, all the beads will pull inwards toward the center. All stitch placements are aimed toward the midpoint of the centre bead.

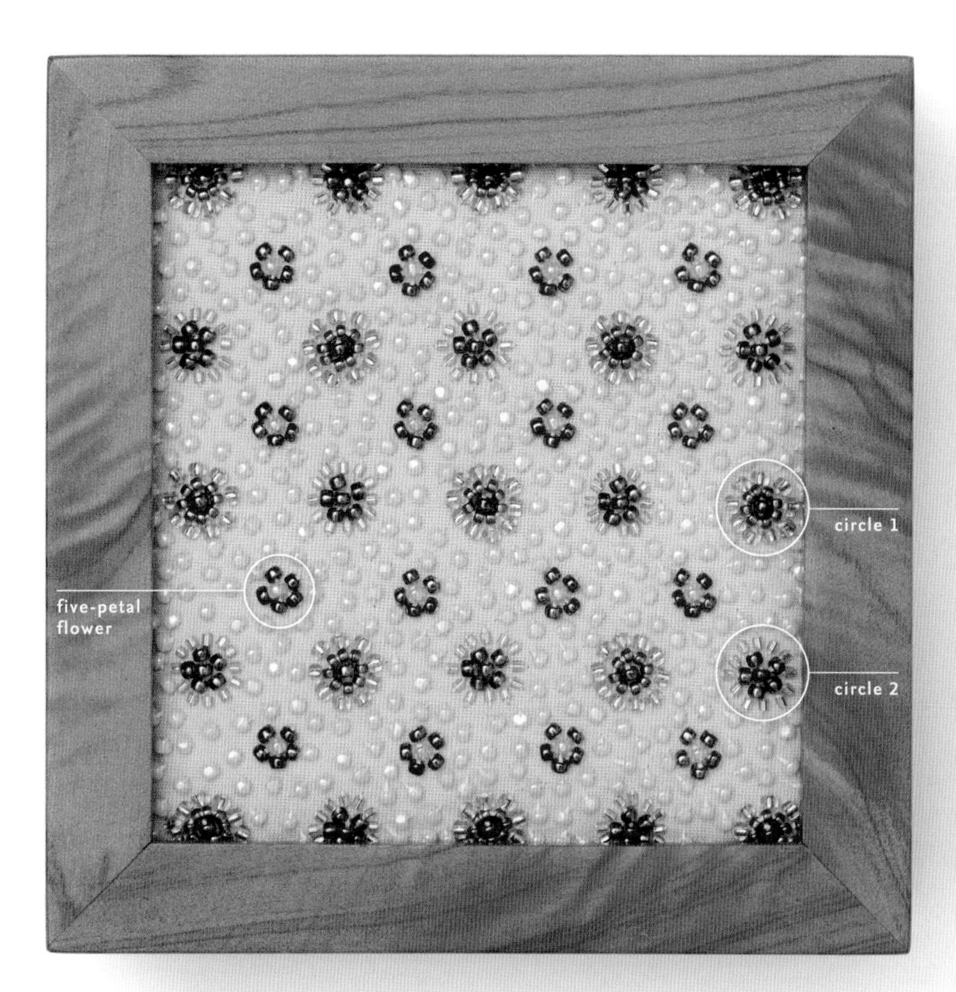

The above sequence of stitches will result in a simple twelve-petal flower with an even distribution of beads that flow within the circle.

FIVE-PETAL FLOWER

Stitch the five-petal flowers in the same manner as the centre of **Circle 2** using **B** for the centre and **D** for the petals.

CONSTRUCTION

On completion of the embroidery, check that the measurements are still correct.

1 ***Complete the finishing process.***

2 Keep the beading on the frame. Measure out the exact box top opening. Using the measurements cut out a piece of fusible thin wadding.

3 Fuse the wadding to the wrong side of the beading. Leave to cool.

4 When cool, remove the work from the frame and cut out adding a 2.5cm (1") seam allowance. Lace the beaded fabric over the cardboard backing ensuring it is a good fit to the box opening.

Most boxes will come with a ready-cut backing. If not, measure and cut a backing from a piece of foam core or acid free white cardboard, available from most art stores.

5 Cut another piece of cardboard. Fit the laced card first then the second piece to hide the lacing and give a nice finish. This step is not necessary if the box comes with a built in backing.

MAGENTA STAR

This single flower was inspired by the *Florentine II* range of quilt fabric designed by Peggy O'Toole for *Robert Kaufmann Fabric*. It reminds me of the stunning mignon dahlia, the Magenta Star and there is no better name to give to this project.

This simple, single flower project introduces ***raised effect techniques***, ***couching technique 1–combination needle-koma method*** for linear and circle effects as well as practice for achieving fine points. This flower decorates a mirror case as well as the back of an accompanying compact mirror. Also shown is the same flower on a different background colour decorating the top of a small trinket box.

Techniques Used

Raised effect–general padding and stitch length adjustment

Couching technique 1–combination needle-koma method

Vertical single layer

Scatter effect technique 1–singles or doubles

Couching technique 2–long straight lines

Learning Points

Planning the embroidery sequence to achieve the best visual aesthetics

Using the ***couching technique 1–combination needle-koma method*** to create a circle and a smooth line

Couching with komas

Creating dimension with:

a) Raised effect by adjusting stitch length

b) Raised effect with padding

c) Tapering a flower through variation of bead colour and size

Achieving neat points

Fabric and supplies

24cm x 25cm wide (9 1/2" x 10") piece of red silk taffeta

14cm x 24cm wide (5 1/2" x 9 1/2") piece of red silk taffeta

25cm (10") square of fusible medium wadding

Matching sewing thread

PVA glue

Mirror compact kit

Gilding pen

Mirror compact kit

Beads

Bead quantities listed refer to a 5cm x 12mm (2" x ½") tube

TOHO SIZE 11 SEED BEADS
A = 241 rainbow
lt topaz/mauve-lined (2/3)
B = 332 gold-lustre dk raspberry (2/3)

TOHO SIZE 15 SEED BEADS
C = 1 clear transparent (1/4)
D = 108B Kelly green transparent lustre (1/3)
E = 241 rainbow
lt topaz/mauve-lined (1/4)
F = 332 gold-lustre dk raspberry (1 1/2)
G = 551 matte galvanized rose-gold (2/3)

PRECIOSA SIZE 12 SEED BEADS
H = ruby lustre (1/3)

PATTERN

For the mirror: Measure the diameter of the circle and re-draw a circle template 1mm (1/32") wider, i.e. the diameter will be 2 mm (1/16") wider.

For the mirror case: The design template measures 19cm x 9.5mm wide (7 1/2" x 3 3/4"). The weft of the fabric lies lengthwise across the template.

DESIGN AND PATTERN PREPARATION

See the liftout pattern for the embroidery design.

Before any embroidery can commence the fabric must be prepared and framed up. Generally this proceeds in the following sequence:

1 Transfer the design to the fabric.

2 Frame up fabric.

3 Place pattern template over the design and outline using ***line of held thread technique***.

Position and transfer the single flower motif in the centre of the circle and 4.25cm (1 3/4") in from the opening edge of the pattern template. With the gilding pen apply random spots of gold throughout the centre of the flower.

PLANNING THE EMBROIDERY SEQUENCE

Reviewing the overall design:

A single flower with eight overlapping petals arranged around a circle. On the outer edge, the sepal tips peep out between the petals. This immediately allows us to separate the design into three distinct sections.

Prioritising the sections:

a) The central circle deserves top priority as it is a shape that must be preserved. If completed first it will not be obstructed by any other stitches

b) There are eight petals. The petals overlap one another so choices need to be made to ensure that the finished embroidery is harmoniously balanced. To this end, I have elected to assign one petal as the dominant petal. In Japanese embroidery, this petal is usually larger than the others and aligned towards the top of the overall design. For the round mirror, no distinction is really necessary but it is appropriate to view the opening end as the top for the mirror case.

c) Begin with this petal and make alternate full petals and the rest as overlapped petals.

d) The tips of the sepals which are behind the petals are worked last. These will abut the petals and fit into the 'v' shape created by the overlapping petals.

In prioritising the embroidery order, we preserve the integrity for all the shapes which make up the design. The infilling parts of these shapes can be completed at any time but the priority sequence of the parts must not be compromised.

ORDER OF WORK

Mirror

1 With the ***couching technique 1–combination needle-koma method***, stitch the circle in the centre of the flower using **G** ensuring that work proceeds in a clockwise direction and stitch direction is from the inside out. The couching stitch should be perpendicular to the thread line of the beads and the couching stitch should hug the thread. Remember the mantra–'Stitch... tension... position'

2 Fill in the circle with ***scatter effect technique 1-singles*** using **G**.

3 Outline the flower petals using **G**. Beginning with the dominant petal complete every alternate petal as a full petal using the ***couching technique 1–combination needle-koma method*** and working in a clockwise direction.

As the petals are overlapped by the circle, it is important to ensure that the end beads of each petal abut the circle without distorting the shape or creating a gap. These are common problems which are caused by incorrect stitch placement. They are easily rectified by ensuring the stitch starts and ends 0.5mm (1/64") from the edge of the bead. Angle the needle straight up or down as it goes through the fabric at these points.

Each petal outline is formed with two lines. To achieve a neat point at the tip of the flower petals, without affecting the integrity of the design lines:

a) At the tip of the petal, stitch the line a half to one bead beyond the tip. This will be determined by how the beads line up but it is important that the last bead goes beyond the point.

b) Pin stitch the bead thread after this first line is complete and this pin stitch should be along the direction of the line.

c) Begin stitching the second line at the point continuing the progression in a clockwise direction. The stitch placement for this starting position of the stitch is critical. The stitch should start on the inside edge and about halfway down the tip of the last bead of the first line. Angle the needle when coming up through the fabric to achieve this. As the second line of beads will be pulled away from the first, this strategic placement of the needle will ensure that the first bead will abut and form a point with the last bead of the first line. If this stitch is not correctly placed, there will be a gap between the two beads and the point will not be achieved.

d) Pin stitch the bead thread after this second line is complete along the direction of the line.

Note: Remember these tips for creating points and achieving good bead positions where design lines abut as they will not be repeated. They are, however, used for all similar design situations for the projects in this book.

---

4 Complete the outline for the remaining background petals using the ***couching technique 1–combination needle-koma method*** as before.

5 Fill in each petal with the aim of achieving the dimensional appearance of a flower in bloom. To this end, technique selection, bead size and colour variation, and padding will be used to give the flower greater dimensional perspective and movement as the beads catch the light at different levels.

An explanation is given below.

a) **Technique for surface stitching:** For a standalone flower, the most logical technique choice will be the ***vertical single layer technique***. When applied to all the petals, the lines simulate the lines of a flower in bloom.

b) **Padding:** To achieve dimensional perspective a decision was made to pad the petals. The outer edge of the petal is more solidly padded than the centre for a tapered effect. This is achieved by stitching the lines of beads abutting each towards the outer edge.

A good guide for this is the point where the petals overlap.

Leave a gap and stitch another line of beads.

Leave the rest of the petals unpadded.

c) **Variation in bead size and colour:** To further emphasise the tapering effect, the size of the beads is reduced towards the centre, naturally drawing the eye. At the same time, deeper colours are used towards the centre of the flower giving the visual illusion of depth.

6 Pad the petals with **C** leaving a one bead space around the edges. Stitch as a ***line of held thread*** horizontally across the petals. Space the horizontal stitches as described above.

7 Complete the surface embroidery for the petals using the ***vertical layer technique***. Begin with a stitch down the centre of the petal using **E** and tapering through **H** to **F**. Do not couch the line of beads. Pin stitch after each stitch back under the same line of beads. This will enhance the raised effect. Complete with similar alternating stitches on either side of this central stitch.

Note: Depending on how your petals are shaped by the outline, there may be some space left to be filled. Do not force a line of beads in place. If necessary, use smaller beads to fill it with a ***rounding stitch****. These stitches will emerge and re-enter the fabric 0.5mm (1/64") in from the outer edge of the preceding line. The pin stitches for the* ***rounding stitch*** *will be made along the direction of the curve.*

---

8 **Sepal tips:** The tips are stitched using **D** and the ***raised effect technique–adjusting stitch length***. Each tip is worked with three stitches. Begin with the stitch down the centre of the shape adding one bead more than required for the line. Only this stitch is raised. Pin stitch back under the same line of beads. Add a stitch on each side of this stitch. Ensure neat points are achieved at both ends by placing the ends of the side stitches at the midpoint under both the first and last stitches.

The pin stitches for these two stitches should follow the direction of the curve.

9 **Background:** The background for the mirror is worked using **F** and ***scatter effect technique 1–singles***. Of the different scatter effect techniques, this gives a relatively more static appearance making a pleasing contrast to the dimensional effects and movement of the central flower.

Mirror Case

1 Using **F** couch an outline of beads with ***couching technique 2–long straight lines*** for the opening of the case. Stitch the first line on the outside of the design line and couch every bead for a firm line.

2 Using **G**, work ***single stitches with one bead***, spaced one bead apart, perpendicular to the beaded outline.

3 Using **F**, couch a second outline of beads using ***couching technique 2–long straight lines***. This line abuts the line of **G** beads. Couch every bead.

4 Complete the flower in the same manner as the mirror.

5 Background: Complete the background using **F** with ***scatter effect –technique 1 doubles***. Double beads are used as the case has a greater surface area to be covered. The double beads give more movement to the background and provide a better overall visual balance.

CONSTRUCTION

Complete the finishing process.

Mirror:

1 Using the template cut a piece of fusible medium wadding. Fuse to the wrong side of the bead embroidery. Remove from the frame and cut out with a 2cm (3/4") seam allowance.

2 Mirror kits usually come with a ready-cut piece of cardboard. If not, cut a piece of cardboard to fit the shape. Fitting instructions should also be provided.

3 Work running stitch 5mm (3/16") in from the raw edge around the beaded piece. Do not end off the thread.

4 Centre the cardboard circle on the wrong side of the beaded fabric and pull up the gathering thread firmly.

Check to ensure that the beading is centred and secure the thread with 3–4 back stitches.

5 Fit the embroidery into the compact mirror using the instructions from the kit.

Mirror case:

1 With the embroidery still on the frame, measure the beaded piece. Using the measurements, cut out :

- Fusible wadding. Trim away 1mm (1/32") from the long sides.
- Fusible wadding for the lining. Trim away 2mm (1/16") across the width and 1cm (3/8") across the length.
- Lining fabric with a 1cm (3/8") seam allowance larger than the lining interfacing. The weft of the fabric should be along the length of the pattern.

2 Fuse the wadding to the wrong side of the beaded piece. Allow to cool.

3 Remove the beaded piece from the frame and cut out, adding a 1cm (3/8") seam allowance. Apply glue to the edge of the seam allowance only. Fold the seam allowance under and glue the seam in position. The folded edge should lie just under the line of beads.

Note: Do not allow the glue to touch the fabric along the folded edge as this will make subsequent stitching difficult.

---

4 Fuse the wadding to the lining fabric. Fold under the seam allowance and tack in place.

5 Sliptitch the lining to the beaded piece making sure that the edges line up at the opening. The lining should be 1mm (1/32") narrower on the long edges and should sit just under the line of beads. The lining is shorter than the beaded piece across the folded length to allow for the fold and padding. Fold in half and check that the lining lines up and fits at the remaining short end. Adjust if necessary. Slipstitch the lining and beaded piece at the second short end and along the long edges. The lining will sit 1mm (1/32") in from the long edges of the beaded piece.

6 Fold the piece in half and join the two side edges with ladder stitch using a double thread for strength. The stitches should catch the fabric directly under the beads.

Use a bulldog clip to hold the sides together while stitching to prevent the edges from slipping.

Reinforce the stitching at the upper edges for added strength. Ensure that the stitches catch the fabric just under the beaded edge.

7 On completion, fold some acid free tissue paper into shape and place inside the case. Steam gently with a wet cloth over an iron or a commercial steamer.

8 Remove the damp tissue and replace with paper. Manipulate the case into shape and let it dry overnight before use.

RHYTHM OF BEADS

There are no complicated techniques in this project. It aims to demonstrate how an effective visual outcome can be achieved using only the most basic stitches, a limited colour palette and small variety of beads.

Techniques Used

Single stitches with one bead

Line of held thread

Japanese running stitch

Scatter effect technique 1 – singles

Learning Points

Understanding stitch direction and spacing

Becoming familiar with the concept of stitch lengths in practice

Using different bead sizes and spacing to create a tapering effect

Choice of bead type, size, finish and colour to create subtle colour shading

Beads are applied singly and only four varieties in different sizes, colours and finishes are used. The main design uses a single bead type and colour in two sizes, strategically stitched to form line patterns.

By using a single bead type, a consistent visual pattern of lines is created. The use of smaller beads at the ends of the lines gives a tapering effect drawing the eye along the flow.

To contrast and complement the pattern lines of single colour, the background is given a subtle shading and texture using two types of beads in different sizes, colour, cut and finish. The opaque, black 3-cut beads provide interest and texture as the light reflects off the cut surfaces. To enhance the textured look, size 15 beads with an iridescent finish are mixed in.

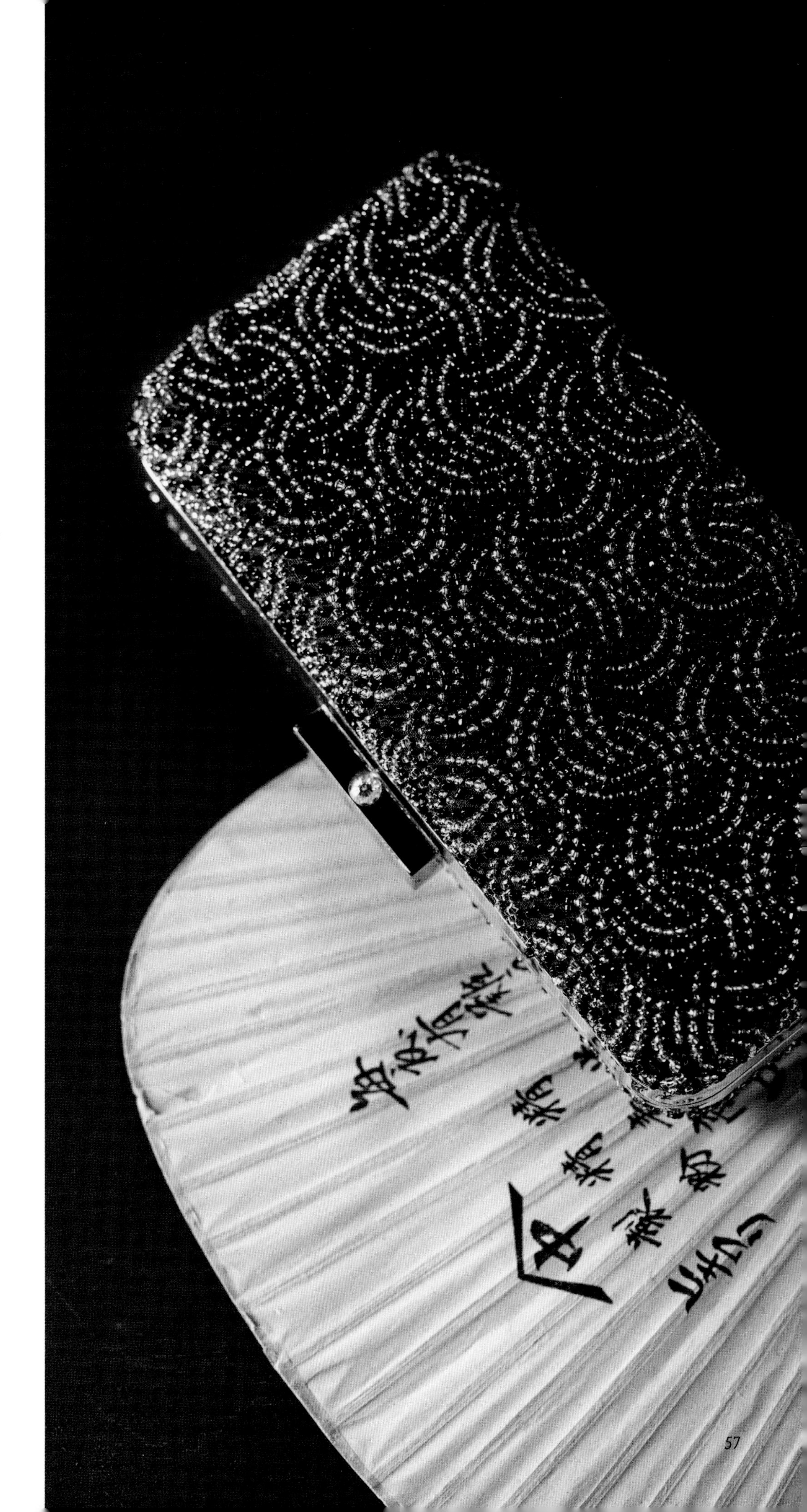

Fabric and supplies

32cm x 25cm wide (13" x 10") piece of dark charcoal cotton quilting fabric or cotton print quilting fabric

15cm x 45cm wide (6" x 18") piece of lining fabric

15cm x 45cm wide (6" x 18") piece of fusible thin wadding

Clamshell purse kit: 18cm x 9cm x 6.5cm deep (7" x 3 1/2" x 2 1/2")

PVA Glue

Multi-use glue suitable for metal

Small, stiff-bristled paint brush

Beads

Bead quantities listed refer to a 5cm x 12mm (2" x 1/2") tube

TOHO SIZE 11 SEED BEADS
A = 22 silver-lined lt gold (1 1/4)

TOHO SIZE 15 SEED BEADS
B = 22 silver-lined lt gold (3/4)
C = 84 metallic moss iris (3/4)

TOHO 3-CUT SIZE 12 BEADS
D = 49 opaque shiny jet black (1 1/2)

DESIGN AND PATTERN PREPARATION

See the liftout pattern for the embroidery design.

Before any embroidery can commence the fabric must be prepared and framed up. Generally this proceeds in the following sequence:

1. Transfer the design to the fabric.
2. Frame up fabric.
3. Place pattern template over the design and outline using ***line of held thread technique***.

ORDER OF WORK

1. Stitch the pattern lines first. For each line, stitch the first bead at the midpoint using **A**. The stitch placement follows the design line and stitch direction for this first bead can be from right to left or left to right along the line.
2. Stitch one side of the divided pattern line in the following manner. Stitch a second bead with the stitch direction inward towards the first bead leaving a spacing of approximately 1mm (1/32") between the stitched beads. This spacing must be maintained for all subsequent stitching. Pay attention to stitch direction, stitch placement and stitch length as any of these, if not properly executed will negatively affect the visual flow of the lines.

Note: Pin stitch after every 2–3 beads. Pin stitch in line with stitch direction.

Continue in the same manner changing to **B** for the last 3–4 beads at the end. Spacing between beads remains unchanged at the spacing established earlier.

3 Repeat for the remaining half of the line.

4 Continue until all lines are complete. Adjust the number of beads as appropriate for the lines. They do not need to be the same and in fact, will have a more relaxed look if they are irregular.

5 When all lines are complete, work the background using a mix of **C** and **D** in ***scatter effect technique 1*** with single beads.

CONSTRUCTION

The clamshell purse consists of a metal frame and two moulded cases that are shaped to fit into the frame. There are concealed fittings in the frame that give the option for attaching a chain, if desired.

Beaded piece

Complete the finishing process. Using the template, check that sizing remains correct and cut a piece of fusible wadding. Fuse the wadding to the back of the beaded piece and remove from the frame. Cut a 2.5cm (1") seam allowance all round. This is generous but will facilitate easier handling at this stage.

Sew darts on the beaded piece using ladder stitch.

Using the paint brush coat the outer side of each half of the plastic case with a thin layer of PVA glue. Do not do anything to the inside of the case at this stage. Gently smooth one piece of the beaded fabric over each side of the case, pulling around the edges to ensure a nice fit. Check the fit against the metal frame. Allow the glue to dry and trim the fabric flush with the edge of the case.

Lining

Cut a piece of lining fabric to fit the inside of each half of the case with a 1cm (3/8") seam allowance. Using the brush apply a thin layer of PVA glue to the inside of each half ensuring that the glue goes right to the edge. On each side of the case position a piece of lining and, beginning at the centre, smooth in place. Trim where necessary.

Apply the multi-use glue into the crevice of the metal frame avoiding the latch and hinge mechanisms. Use a toothpick to spread the glue evenly. Fit the cases into the metal frame and push on both sides to ensure that they are fitted neatly and firmly in place. Allow the glue to dry thoroughly, preferably overnight, before using.

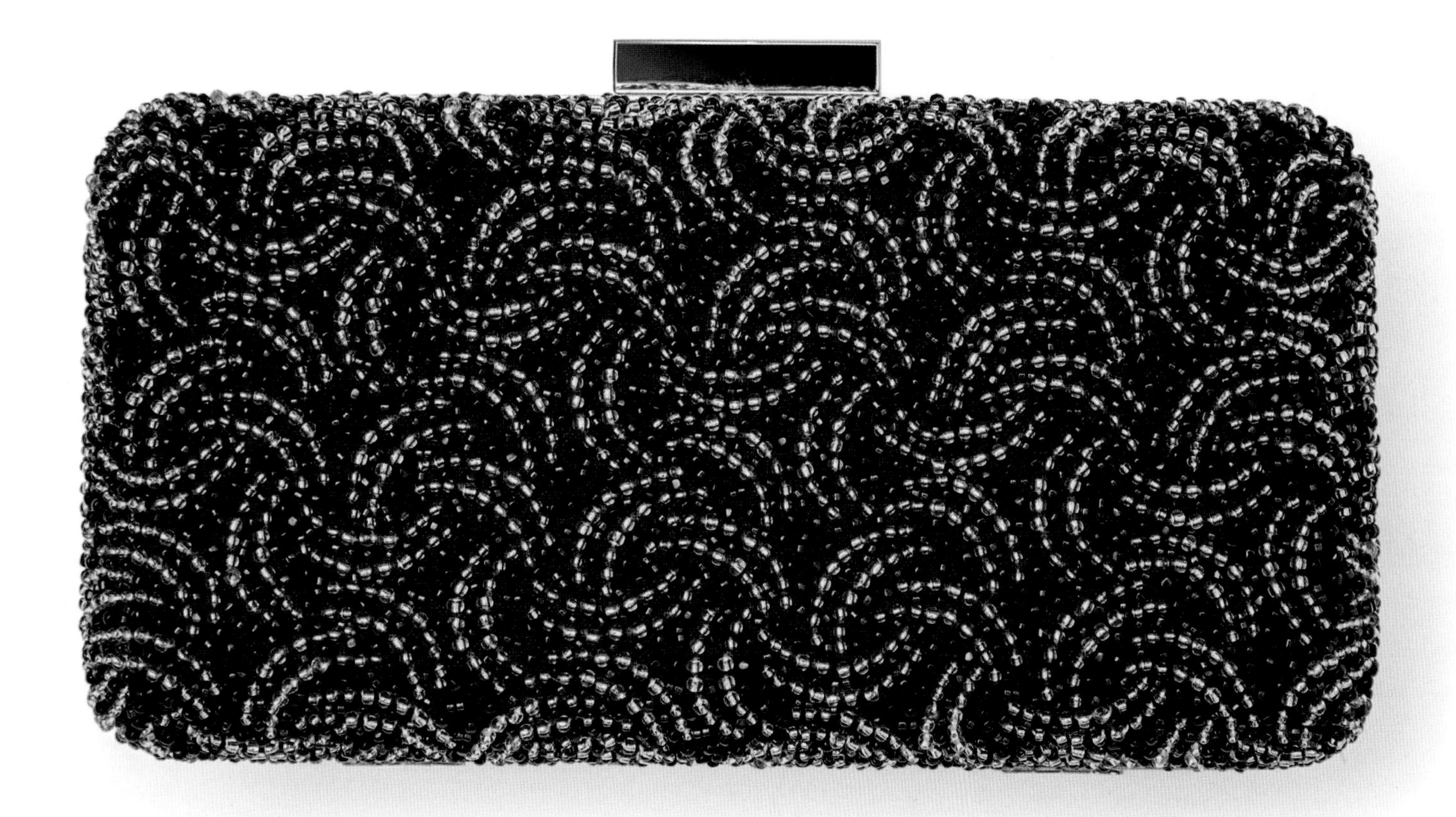

YULETIDE

Yuletide is designed to evoke the spirit of Christmas and decorates a box top. Add a little something to the box and it will make a Christmas gift for someone special. In this project, crystals have been used to create a highlight within the design.

Techniques Used

Single stitches with one bead

Line of held thread

Raised effect–padding and stitch length adjustment

Couching technique 1–combination needle-koma method

Stamen effect

Separated single layer combined with raised effect

Scatter effect technique 1–singles

Scatter effect technique 2–singles and doubles

Learning Points

Planning the embroidery sequence to achieve the best visual aesthetics for the design

Using the needle-koma method to achieve smooth lines around tight curves

Managing multiple elements within a motif

Maintaining design balance

Creating dimensional perspective

Achieving neat points

Fabric and supplies

24cm x 26cm (9 1/2" x 10 1/4") piece of mottled yellow quilting cotton

12cm x 16cm wide (4 3/4" x 6 3/8") piece of fusible thin wadding

Rectangular wooden box with a 10cm x 16cm wide (4" x 6 1/4") opening

Beads

Bead quantities listed refer to a 5cm x 12mm (2" x 1/2") tube

TOHO SIZE 11 SEED BEADS
A = 22 silver-lined lt gold (1/8)
B = 177 smoky topaz rainbow (1/8)

TOHO SIZE 15 SEED BEADS
C = 1 clear transparent (1/8)
D = 5B Siam ruby (1/2)
E = 22 silver-lined lt gold (1/3)
F = 108B Kelly green transparent lustre (1/8)
G = 162B medium topaz rainbow (1/8)
H = 177 smoky topaz rainbow (1/8)
I = 221 bronze metallic (1/3)

TOHO SIZE 12 3-CUT BEADS
J = 5B Siam ruby (2/3)
K = 103 transparent gold rainbow (1)
L = 108 Kelly green (1/8)
M = 123 opaque lustre lt beige (1/8)
N = 932 dk blue-lined lt blue (1/8)

PRECIOSA SIZE 9 3-CUT BEADS
O = red AB (2/3)

SWAROVSKI CRYSTAL 4MM
P = 001 AB (1 piece)
Q = 237 fire opal (3 pieces)

SWAROVSKI MARGUERITE CRYSTAL 6MM
R = vitrail (3 pieces)

DESIGN AND PATTERN PREPARATION

See the liftout pattern for the embroidery design.

Before any embroidery can commence the fabric must be prepared and framed up. Generally this proceeds in the following sequence:

1 Transfer the design to the fabric.

2 Frame up fabric.

3 Place pattern template over the design and outline using ***line of held thread technique***.

The design is rectangular in shape. The corners are marked on the design. Use these as a guide to mark out the project.

ORDER OF WORK

Central Flower

1 Begin with the star shape outline using the ***line of held thread*** method and **E**. Work carefully to achieve neat points and corners.

2 Outline the full foreground petals. Identify the prominent petal and stitch this and alternate petals as full foreground petals. Begin each outline at the tip with **D**, change to **O** and taper the line towards the centre with the smaller beads, using ***couching technique 1–combination needle-koma method***.

3 Work the background petals in a similar fashion to the full petals with the same beads.

4 Stitch the centre line of each petal using the ***line of held thread technique*** with **A** tapering to **E** at each end. The stitch direction is inward aimed towards the midpoint of the flower. Tie down every bead.

5 Fill each petal with ***separated single layer technique*** using **J** and **D**. Begin and end each stitch with **D**. Adjust the number of beads used and the size to fit the available space. Create a slight ***raised effect*** towards the points of the petals by adjusting the length of the stitch and pin stitching back under the stitches. Do not overcrowd these stitches or the shape of the petals will be distorted.

6 Stitch the bud shapes in between the petals using **A** and **E**. These are stitched in the same way as the sepal tips in the MAGENTA STAR project. In this instance a round tip is the aim. This is achieved by adjusting bead sizes. For the centre raised stitch begin with **A** tapering to **E**. Work the two side stitches, using **E** at both ends and **A** in the centre of each stitch.

7 Stitch a stem to join the bud shape to the flower with a line of beads, using **I**, worked with the ***line of held thread technique***. This line of beads abuts the bud shape and ends in the corner where the petals join. Work the calyx with a stitch of three beads on each side of the bud joining to the stem line.

8 Using **B** and **H** work the three stitches at the tips of each petal beginning with the centre stitch. These beads lie flat and are pin stitched along the line after each stitch. Taper the stitches at each end with the smaller beads.

9 Complete the flower with an outline of beads using the ***line of held thread technique***. Begin with **A** at the tip of the petal tapering through **E** to **I**.

10 The centre of the flower is worked when all other beading is complete.

Corner motifs and small flowers

Large side view flower

1 Begin with the calyx which is made up of three stitches. Begin with the centre stitch and position the two outer stitches on each side using **L** and tapering to a point at the base with **F**. The centre stitch may be slightly raised by pin stitching back under the stitch.

2 Begin stitching petals with the two centre stitches. Use one **O** bead on the tip and **D** for the remainder. All stitches are worked from the outer edge towards the base. Tie down the lines if desired.

3 Add a row of spaced single beads using **E** above the outer edge of the flower. Keep a consistent space equivalent to a size 11 bead from the petal tips.

Main stem

Working in a clockwise direction, stitch the main stem using **I** with ***couching technique 1–combination needle-koma method***.

Small side view flower

1 Stitch this in the same way as the large flower adjusting the number of beads for the shape. Tie down the calyx as the last step after the complete flower has been stitched. This will ensure that the bead lines lie effectively without crowding into each other.

2 Using **I** work the stem and abut it to the main stem using the ***line of held thread technique***.

3 Stitch the small side twigs with ***single stitches*** toward the main stem using **I**.

Shaped leaves

1 Begin by outlining the leaves with **I**. The two shorter lines are stitched using the ***line of held thread–curved lines technique*** while the longer line is stitched using ***couching technique 1–combination needle-koma method***.

2 Stitch the leaf veins using the ***line of held thread technique*** with **B** and **H**.

3 Fill the leaves with ***scatter effect technique 3–solid random*** using **C**.

Curled stem

1 Stitch the curled stem using ***couching technique 1–combination needle-koma method*** working in a clockwise direction using **I**. Couch between every bead.

2 Add single **N** beads spaced along the outer edge at the positions marked. Angle the beads diagonally to the stem.

3 Complete the motif with single lines of green beads using **F**.

Small five-petal flowers

Stitch these flowers using **M** for the centre bead and **O** for the petals.

Simple small leaves

These are worked in two ways:

1 A single line of beads using the ***line of held thread technique*** and **F**.

2 Two lines of beads, also using **F**. These are stitched in the following sequence for the best results.

a) Identify the leading line for the leaf. This is usually the outer curve. Stitch a line with the appropriate number of beads.

b) Stitch a second line for the remaining side. Pay attention to the stitch placement to ensure clean points are achieved on both ends.

c) Tie down the stitches using the ***line of held thread technique*** for the final shaping.

Background

The background is completed with ***scatter effect technique 2–singles and doubles*** using **K**. This light-coloured transparent bead allows the mottled colour of the fabric to show through adding another dimension.

Central flower motif centre

This is worked last as the elements here are raised and have the potential to snag stitches.

For added effect and highlights, *Swarovski* crystals are used here and are worked using the ***stamen effect technique.***

a) Begin with the center stitch using **P** with **G** at the tip.

b) Work the next three stitches equally spaced around the central using **Q** with **G** at the tip

c) Add three more stitches using **R** with **G** at the tip.

Complete the section with ***scatter effect technique 1-singles*** using **G**.

CONSTRUCTION

Complete the finishing process.

Insert the beaded panel in the same manner as the CIRCLES project using a larger 5cm (2") seam allowance.

FLORAL PARADE

This is an interesting study as all the main flowers are stitched in a similar way and depend on the use of bead size, technique and design concepts to create visual dimension. Some gilding and embroidery with metal threads are also used to add another dimension to the design.

As there are many similar elements within the design, colour choices and their distribution are important factors for balance and flow.

Techniques Used

Single stitches with one bead

Raised effect–stitch length adjustment

Line of held thread

Line of held thread–circle method

Line of held thread–curved lines

Vertical single layer

Separated single layer

Scatter effect technique 2–singles and doubles

Line of staggered diagonals with metallic thread

Alternate vertical–horizontal technique

Learning Points

Planning the embroidery sequence to achieve the best visual aesthetics

Creating dimension for adjoining motifs stitched with the same basic technique

Achieving a harmonious flow for ***separated single layer technique***
All the leaves are worked with this technique but there are differences in orientation and curves

Creating a balance in colour and design

Combining other techniques with bead embroidery

Completing a beaded outline of the project

Fabric and supplies

23cm (9") square of deep teal quilting cotton

23cm (9") square of black quilting cotton

20cm x 40cm wide (8" x 16") piece of fusible thin wadding

20cm (8") square of fusible medium interfacing

Gilding pen

PVA glue

Beads and thread

Bead quantities listed refer to a 5cm x 12mm (2" x 1/2") tube

TOHO SIZE 11 SEED BEADS
A = 22 silver-lined lt gold (1/4)
B = 35 silver-lined sapphire (1/4)
C = 162B transparent rainbow medium topaz (1/3)
D = 356 lt amethyst/fuchsia-lined (1/3)
E = 779 rainbow crystal/salmon-lined (1/3)

TOHO SIZE 15 SEED BEADS
F = 5B Siam ruby (1/3)
G = 21 silver-lined crystal (1/4)
H = 22 silver-lined lt gold (1/4)
I = 28 silver-lined cobalt (1/4)
J = 162C transparent rainbow dk topaz (1/4)
K = 188 rainbow crystal slate blue-lined (2/3)
L = 205 gold-lustre dk amethyst (1/4)
M = 241 rainbow lt topaz/mauve-lined (1/4)
N = 284 metallic green-lined aqua (1)
O = 457 gold-lustre green tea (1)
P = 779 rainbow crystal/salmon-lined (1/3)

TOHO SIZE 12 3-CUT BEADS
Q = 49 opaque jet black (1 1/2)
R = 123 opaque lustre lt beige (1/3)
S = 290 transparent lustre rose (1/3)
T = 421 transparent gold-lustre pink (1/4)

TOHO SIZE 15 3-CUT BEADS
U = 179 transparent rainbow emerald (1/4)
V = 421 transparent gold-lustre pink (1/4)

PRECIOSA SIZE 9 3-CUT BEADS
W = red AB (1/3)

METAL THREAD
X = no.1 Jap gold

DESIGN AND PATTERN PREPARATION

See the liftout pattern for the embroidery design.

Before any embroidery can commence the fabric must be prepared and framed up. Generally this proceeds in the following sequence:

1 Transfer the design to the fabric.
2 Frame up fabric.
3 Place pattern template over the design and outline using ***line of held thread technique.***

ORDER OF WORK

Begin with the flowers that are grouped working from the largest to the smallest. Where flowers are the same size, work the foreground flower first.

The petals are all stitched in a similar manner with slight variations. The common methodology for stitching the flowers is given below. This will be followed by the variations for each different flower and instructions for completion.

Remember the pin stitch directions as this will be a critical factor in the overall outcome for the different flowers.

1 All flower centres are stitched with either a single bead or a single bead encircled with beads using the ***line of held thread-circle method.*** For ease of reference, the latter will be referred to as ***encircled bead method*** for the remaining instructions.
2 Petals are stitched using a combination of different numbers of beads (2–7) depending on the size of the flower.
3 Begin with stitches in the north-south direction with the appropriate number of beads positioning size 11 beads on the outer and size 15 beads on the inner edges.
4 Work stitches in the same manner in an east-west direction.
5 Add the appropriate number of stitches equally distributed in the remaining spaces to complete the flower. When working the larger flowers, the space is further divided by stitches placed in a NE, SW, NW and SE direction.
6 All stitches are directed inwards towards the flower centre. Pin stitch along the line of the stitch direction. Tie down stitches where appropriate. If the petals are worked to create a raised effect, no tie-down stitches are necessary.
7 Apply gilding to the flower centres as indicated.

Flower 1: Large red flower

This flower is given prominence with the use of bright colour that has a comparatively greater contrast with the background, and the use of ***raised effect.***

Each flower is formed by alternating raised and flat stitches, and this, in combination with bead choice, creates dimension and movement.

1 Stitch the flower center with the ***encircled bead method*** using either **R** or **B** for the centre bead and **H** for the circle.
2 Work the petals at the north, south, east and west positions using the ***raised effect-stitch length adjustment method.*** Each stitch is made with three **W** beads and the required number of **F** beads plus two extra. Work each stitch to abut the flower centre and pin stitch back under the bead line.
3 Between the cardinal points, divide each segment into thirds and work two petals in each space in the same manner.
4 Between each of these, work a petal using two **W** beads and 2–3 **F** beads.

   These are regular stitches that lie flat to the fabric and do not extend to the centre of the flower. They fit between the raised stitches as far as the space permits.

   The flat stitches are all tied down two beads in from the edge of the stitches. Work around the flower in a back stitch fashion.

Flower 2: Large pink flower

Although the largest in their respective group, these flowers are worked differently to **Flower 1**. Instead of a gradual colour transition as the petals converge towards the centre, colour variation helps define the flower.

1 The flower center is stitched with the ***encircled bead method*** using **R** or **B** for the centre bead and **H**.

2 The petals are stitched flat with sixteen stitches. Each stitch has two or three **E** beads on the outer and two **M** beads towards the centre. Use three **E** beads for the larger pink flower and two for the smaller one. Tie down with one stitch at the midpoint if desired.

Flower 3: Medium flowers with raised petals

1 The centre of the mauve flower is stitched with the encircled bead method using **R** or **B** for the centre bead and **H** for the circle. When working the blue flower, gild a 4mm (5/32") circle and stitch a single **R** bead at the centre.

2 The sixteen petals are stitched with a hint of ***raised effect***. The stitch length is only slightly shortened. Each stitch has two size 11 beads on the outer and two to three size 15 beads towards the centre, depending on the size of the flower.

Note: Depending on individual stitch placements, the number of petals may need to be increased or reduced by one. All stitches are pin stitched back under the stitch just worked.

*The mauve flower is stitched with **D** and **L**.*

*The blue flower uses **B** and **I**. The petal stitches do not join the centre bead. Leave a 1mm (1/32") gap between the end of each petal and the centre bead. The gilding will show in the gap giving the flower a different dimension.*

Flower 4: Medium flowers with flat petals

These are the remaining multi-petal flowers not allocated a reference number in the stitching guide. They are stitched in the same way as **Flower 3** but with regular stitches. They include the following variations:

1. When working the yellow flowers, a coat of gilding is first applied to the full flower circle shape. This intensifies the colour as the darker background fabric does not show between the stitches.
2. Work the flower centres with ***single stitches with one bead*** or the ***encircled bead method***.
3. Petals are worked up to the centre beads or with a space. Note that a flower stitched with a space without gilding has the effect of visually receding the flower centre.
4. The number of beads used for each petal can be two, three or four with the larger sized beads placed on the outer edge and smaller beads towards the centre to taper the line.
5. The number of stitches making up the petals is adjusted accordingly to fit the space and ranges from eight to sixteen.
6. Stitches can be tied down if desired or left untied for a more relaxed look.
7. Bead combinations for the various flowers are:

   Flower centres
   Single beads of **A**, **B**, **R** or **W**
   Encircled beads using **R** and **H** or **W** and **K**

   Petals
   B and **I**
   W and **F**
   D and **L**
   E and **P**
   C and **J**

Side View Flowers

These vary in size and are evenly distributed between the clusters of three flowers. To maintain visual balance, these are stitched with a combination of ***raised effect*** and regular stitches.

1. Begin with the calyx using **O** and working three stitches for the larger flowers and a single bead aligned with the stem for the smaller flowers.
2. Stitch the flower petals next starting with the centre then working one side and then the other. All flower petals are stitched using **S** and **E** on the outer edge and tapering with **P** towards the calyx. Only one **S** bead is used in any one stitch.

   On the larger flowers, the stitches are alternately raised and flat. These are worked in the same way as **Flower 1**, with the raised stitches completed first then fitting the regular flat stitches in between.

   The smaller flowers with four or five petals may include one or two petals stitched with ***raised effect*** but the smaller flowers with three petals are stitched with regular flat stitches. Tie down the outer two stitches, if necessary, to attain the desired flower shape.

Flower sprig 1 and small bronze flowers

Each of the flowers are individually stitched using the ***encircled bead method***. The smaller flowers use **R** for the centre and **V** for the circle and the larger flowers use **R** for the centre and **T** for the circle.

Flower Sprig 2

1. Stitch two lines of beads to form a 'v' shape using **U**. Pay attention to achieving a neat point. Do not tie down at this stage.
2. Between the 'v', work a vertical stitch using either a single **W** bead or one **W** and one **F** bead together.
3. Tie down the stitches of the 'v' to shape.

Leaves

All the leaves are stitched with the ***separated single layer technique***.

Leaves have either a smooth or a serrated outline. Ensure these are maintained through accurate placement of stitches especially on the outer edge.

Pay attention to the curve of the leaves. On the convex side of the leaf the spaces between the stitches are slightly further apart to follow the line of the curve.

Similarly, the stitches on the outer edge of the concave side are brought closer together.

Maintain a relatively steep angle for the stitches to generate 'movement'.

1. Begin with a line of beads stitched using the ***line of held thread technique*** for the smaller leaves and the ***couching technique 1–combination needle-koma method*** for the larger leaves. Tie down or couch between every bead. This represents the centre vein line.
2. Work diagonal stitches down one side of the leaf. It is preferable to begin with the concave side. Work these stitches from the tip down. Pay attention to the curve of the leaf and adjust the placement of the stitches to complement it. Stitches are from the outer edge in towards the center vein. Pin stitch after every stitch along the stitch direction line.
3. Complete the second side in a similar fashion.
4. Where required, complete with tie-down stitches to complete the final shaping for the leaf.

The leaves are stitched using three main colours. The larger leaves are stitched in blue to create interest and also to break up the distribution of the green.

For the green, two complementary colours have been selected. The first is a subtle shade of gold-lustre green. This is an all-time favourite as it always seems to pick up and tone with most surrounding colours. It is a most useful colour to keep handy in your stash. They are a bit more pricey but are truly worth it.

The other bead is an 'inside colour' bead with a transparent light aqua outer and a metallic green inner, which produces an interesting greenish tinge. Being transparent, the outer edges of the bead also blend with the ground fabric. Colour selection for each leaf is made on the premise of achieving overall balance and harmony. See the FAQs section for tips on this subject.

Beads used:
Blue leaves: **G** and **K**
Green leaves 1: **N** and **H**
Green leaves 2: **O** and **H**

Stems

After completing the flowers, the stems are stitched with **X** using the Japanese embroidery technique called ***line of staggered diagonals*** (see page 95). The three-step technique is used for the finer stem and the four step technique for the thicker stem.

The thread is half hitched, which means that the embroidery is done with a pair of threads.

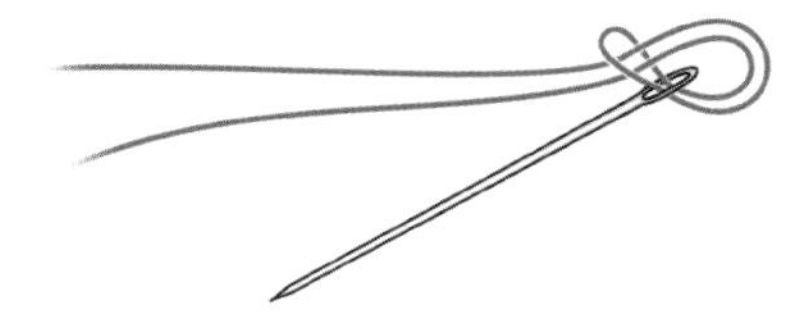

Single White Flowers

These flowers are not marked on the design and their placement will be dependent on how the bead embroidery for the other elements has turned out and how much space there is. Scatter them and use them to break up adjoining colours or lines.

You may elect to be guided by the stitched project shown or by personal preference. These small five-petal flowers are stitched in the standard way using **A** for the centre and **R** for the five petals.

Background

Complete the bead embroidery by stitching the background using ***scatter effect technique 2–singles and doubles*** with **Q**.

CONSTRUCTION

1 ***Complete the finishing process.***

2 With the work still on the frame, measure the beaded piece. Using the measurements cut out:

a) Fusible thin wadding–Trim away 2mm (1/16") from each long edge. Check against the beaded piece.

b) Fusible medium interfacing. Trim away 2mm (1/16") from each long edge. Check against the beaded piece.

Using the lining pattern piece cut out:

c) Fusible thin wadding

d) Lining fabric with a 1cm (3/8") seam allowance. The weft of the fabric should be along the width of the pattern.

3 Fuse the wadding to the back of the beaded piece. Fuse the interfacing to the wadding. Allow to cool.

4 Remove the beaded piece from the frame and cut out with a 1cm (3/8") seam allowance. Clip the curved edges. Apply glue to the edge of the seam allowance only. Fold the seam allowance under and press in place. The folded edge should lie just under the line of beads.

Note: Do not allow the glue to touch the fabric along the folded edge as it will make subsequent stitching difficult.

---

5 Fuse the wadding to the wrong side of the lining fabric. Fold under the seam allowance and glue or tack in place as before.

6 Attach the lining to the beaded piece making sure that the edges line up. The lining should be slightly smaller than the beaded cover to allow for the fold. Fit the rounded edges of the beaded piece and lining together first. Beginning at the midpoint slipstitch the lining to the beaded piece along one side. When complete return to the centre and repeat for the remaining side.

7 Fit the lining to the remaining three sides ensuring that there are no creases and slipstitch in place.

Note: Greater accuracy will be achieved if this is stitched with the pieces folded over. This is cumbersome but well worth the effort.

8 Fold the piece in half aligning the edges and stitch together with ladder stitch using a doubled thread.

Use a bulldog clip to hold the sides together while stitching. Begin at the base and finish at the opening. At the corner, reinforce the stitching for added strength. Ensure that the stitches are made just under the beaded edge as the beading should finish as close together as possible.

9 On completion, crumple acid-free tissue paper and place inside the case. Manipulate the tissue until the desired shape is achieved. Steam the piece with a wet cloth over a dry iron or a commercial steamer.

10 Remove the wet tissue and replace with fresh dry tissue. Check that the project is still in the desired shape. Reshape, if necessary, by manipulating the fresh tissue. Leave to dry overnight before use.

This project illustrates how a single colour can create effective design movement through variations in stitch technique and bead type.

Techniques Used

Diagonal single layer

Separated single layer

Long and short stitch

Couching technique 1–combination needle-koma method

Couching technique 3–to and fro

Couching technique 4–round and round

Scatter effect technique 1–singles

Learning Points

Planning the embroidery sequence to achieve the best visual aesthetics

Using various couching and stitch techniques to create movement

Combining techniques to create balance

Varying bead types and techniques to create design division

Fabric and supplies

Two pieces each 36cm x 35cm wide (14 1/4" x 14") of black silk taffeta

19cm (7 1/2") kisslock purse frame with stitch holes

30cm x 55cm wide (12" x 22") piece of fusible thin wadding

30cm x 26cm (12" x 10 1/4") piece of fusible heavy interfacing

30cm x 26cm (12" x 10 1/4") piece of fusible medium interfacing

Black quilting thread

PVA glue

Multi-use glue suitable for metal

Fabric adhesive

Beads

Bead quantities listed refer to a 5cm x 12mm (2" x 1/2") tube

TOHO SIZE 11 SEED BEADS
A = 85 metallic iris purple

TOHO SIZE 15 SEED BEADS
B = 85 metallic iris purple

TOHO SIZE 12 3-CUT BEADS
C = 85 metallic iris purple

TOHO 3MM BUGLE BEADS
D = 85 metallic iris purple

TOHO SIZE 12 HEXAGON BEADS
E = 85 metallic iris purple

DESIGN AND PATTERN PREPARATION

Before any embroidery can commence the fabric must be prepared and framed up. Generally this proceeds in the following sequence:

1 Transfer the design to the fabric.

2 Frame up fabric.

3 Place pattern template over the design and outline using ***line of held thread technique***.

The beading is worked onto one piece of the taffeta and the remaining piece is used for the lining. The pattern template consists of a rectangular shape 26cm x 19.5 cm wide (10 1/4" x 7 3/4") and two side pieces. Mark out the main rectangular shape and the side pieces with the ***line of held thread technique.*** The pattern for the side pieces is provided.

ORDER OF WORK

Feather Shapes

1 Begin with the foreground shape working progressively to the background shape. The foreground shape is worked in the ***separated single layer technique*** using **A** and tapering where appropriate with **B**.

2 Fill the centre using the following three patterns. Fill the space with the stitch patterns as dictated by the available space.

a) 3 stitch pattern: Make a single straight stitch with **D** and **B**. Add a **D** bead on each side set at an angle.

b) 2 Stitch pattern: Make the first stitch set at an angle with **D** and **B**. Add a second stitch mirroring the angle of the first stitch and aimed to the midpoint of the **B** bead.

c) Single stitch pattern: This is a single stitch with one **D** bead.

3 The next and subsequent background feather shapes are stitched using the long and short stitch technique using **A** and tapering with **B** towards the inside. The number and size of beads will vary and will be dictated by the available space. Pin stitch after every stitch back under the stitch to create the hint of a ***raised effect***. Do not tie down the stitches.

a) Begin with a stitch down the centre of the feather shape.

b) Stitch alternate ***long and short stitches*** down one side. Although stitching in ***long and short stitches***, note that the stitch placement and angle of the stitches are the same as if it was stitched in the ***separated single layer technique***.

c) On completion for the first side, return to the midpoint and complete the remaining side in the same manner.

d) Only one row of stitches is required for each section. Fill in the gaps with ***scatter effect technique 1–singles***. Keep the spacing fairly loose.

Note: Spacing is an important factor. Do not overcrowd the stitches or the flow of the feather shape will be negatively impacted.

Defining sections within the design

Following the stitching guide (page 78), work the red lines indicated using ***couching technique 1–combination needle-koma method*** or ***couching technique 2–to and fro***. The dense red areas indicate where two or more lines will abut.

- Use ***couching technique 1–needle-koma method*** if the line being stitched is a shorter line or a single independent line.
- Where the lines end up meeting each other or are a distance 1cm (3/8") or less apart, use ***couching technique 2–to and fro***.

- When the first line is complete, couch the bead line at 2mm (1/16") intervals to the start of the next line and continue couching. For this, do some forward planning and start at positions where the lines are further apart and the turns are at the narrower points.

Hints on filling sections

Once the outlines are stitched, clear sections are visible and decisions need to be made as to the beads and the techniques to be applied. These decisions will be based on:

- Flow of design. The dominant feather shapes set the tone for the flow. Decisions on technique choices for all other sections must be made in relation to these.
- Creating areas of visual interest within the design flow.
- Density: Maintaining balance between solidly and lightly filled areas.

Filling the sections

The stitching chart (page 78) indicates the different techniques used in the sample project. You may follow this or adapt it to individual taste. Here is an opportunity to experiment.

1 Stitch the areas indicated using the ***diagonal single layer technique*** first using **A** and **B** where required. Use of left or right diagonal is indicated in the design line and selection is based on maintaining continuity in the design flow.

2 Fill in the solid areas with ***round and round*** lines or ***to and fro*** lines.

a) Where the space is encapsulated and has tapered ends, lines of ***round and round*** couching will give better balance to the section and give emphasis to the shape.

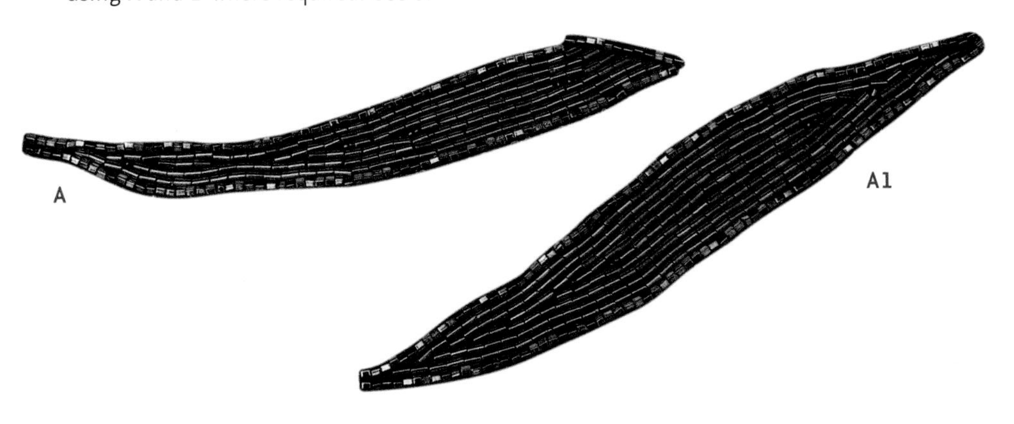

b) Where the space is encapsulated but a section appears to be overlapped by an adjoining area, to and fro lines will give this section a softer and more natural appearance.

In this area, both techniques are used. Beginning from the overlapped end, couching commences and continues as a ***round and round*** line working around the tapered end and back down the other side of the of the area. When it reaches the overlapped point, the couching turns back as a ***to and fro*** line and works its way back as ***round and round*** until it reaches the overlapped end again and turns as a ***to and fro*** line. Couching continues in this manner until the space is filled.

A comparison of Section A and A1 offers an example of how technique choices can affect the flow of the design.

3 Lightly beaded areas: These areas are completed using the ***scatter effect technique 1–singles.*** **C** and **D** beads are used to help maintain the flow of the design better and create areas of visual interest.

a) **D** beads are applied to areas that help maintain or follow through the feather designs. Being longer, these beads also create more texture and give these areas more visual prominence.

b) The remaining areas are stitched with **C**. The 3-cut beads are a better choice than round beads as the additional sparkle from the surface will highlight these areas in a subtle and complementary manner within the overall design.

Random scattered stitches are not always the easiest to do as they seem to have a sneaky way of lining up and forming patterns of their own accord. It seems even more so with bugle beads. One way to circumvent this is to form angles with the beads as you stitch avoiding parallel lines.

Sides

The sides of the bag are completed with ***scatter effect technique I–singles*** using **A**.

CONSTRUCTION

1 ***Complete the finishing process.***

2 With the beading still on the frame, measure the beaded piece and check that the size remains true. Using the measurements, cut out:

a) Backing for the beaded pieces:

i. Fusible thin wadding for the main piece and sides of the bag

ii. Fusible heavy interfacing for the main piece only

i. and ii. Should both be cut to an exact fit plus 5mm (3/16") on the opening edges. Trim 1mm (1/32") from each long edge. Check against the bead piece to ensure the fit is 1mm (1/32") in from both the long edges.

b) Fusible medium interfacing:

Cut to an exact fit lengthwise and trim 4mm (5/32") from each long edge. Use the template for the side pieces and cut to the exact size.

c) Lining fabric using the interfacing as a template and adding a 1cm (3/8") seam allowance on each side. The weft of the fabric should be along the length of the pattern.

3 Fuse the thin wadding then the fusible heavy interfacing to the back of the main piece and the thin wadding and fusible medium interfacing to the back of the side pieces. Allow to cool.

4 When cool, remove the beaded pieces from the frame and cut out with a 1cm (3/8") seam allowance.

Clip the rounded edges for the side pieces. Apply PVA glue to the edge of the seam allowance only. Fold under the seam allowance and glue in position. The folded edge should lie just under the line of beads.

Note: Do not allow the glue to touch the fabric along the folded edge as it will make stitching difficult.

---

5 Fuse the medium interfacing to the back of the lining fabric.

6 Stitching the bag pieces together.

a) Attach the side pieces to the main beaded piece with a double thread and ladder stitch. Begin at the midpoint and work up towards the opening.

Use a bulldog clip to hold the sides together while stitching to prevent the edges from slipping. Stitch until 5mm (3/16") from the end and reinforce the stitches.

b) Return to the midpoint and repeat for the remaining edge.

c) Repeat for the second side.

7 Stitching the lining: This can be done in two ways:

a) The lining is constructed in the same way as the beaded piece except that the pieces are sewn together with right sides facing with small back stitches. Trim to a 2mm (1/16") seam allowance from the outer stitch line and reinforce the cut edges with fabric adhesive.

b) Alternatively, machine stitch the seams together reinforcing with a second line of stitching close to the first. Trim to a 1mm (1/32") allowance from the outer stitch line and reinforce the cut edges with fabric adhesive.

8 Fitting the bag to the frame:

a) Trim the seam allowance on the upper edge to 7mm (5/16") above the bead line. Apply multi-use glue to the edge of the seam allowance, no more than 2mm (1/16") in from the edge.

b) Fit the edge of the beaded bag into the slot of the bag frame so that the edge of the frame butts right up against the beaded edge. No unbeaded fabric should show. Leave until the glue is set.

c) Using the quilting cotton, stitch the bag to the frame through the holes in a running stitch motion going up and down through each hole.

d) Using the same thread and starting from one end of the frame, bring the needle up through the first hole in the frame. Pick up a **C** bead and re-enter the same hole.

e) Continue in the same manner for every hole along the frame.

f) Repeat steps (a) – (e) for the second side. The top edge of the side pieces is unfinished at this stage.

STITCHING GUIDE

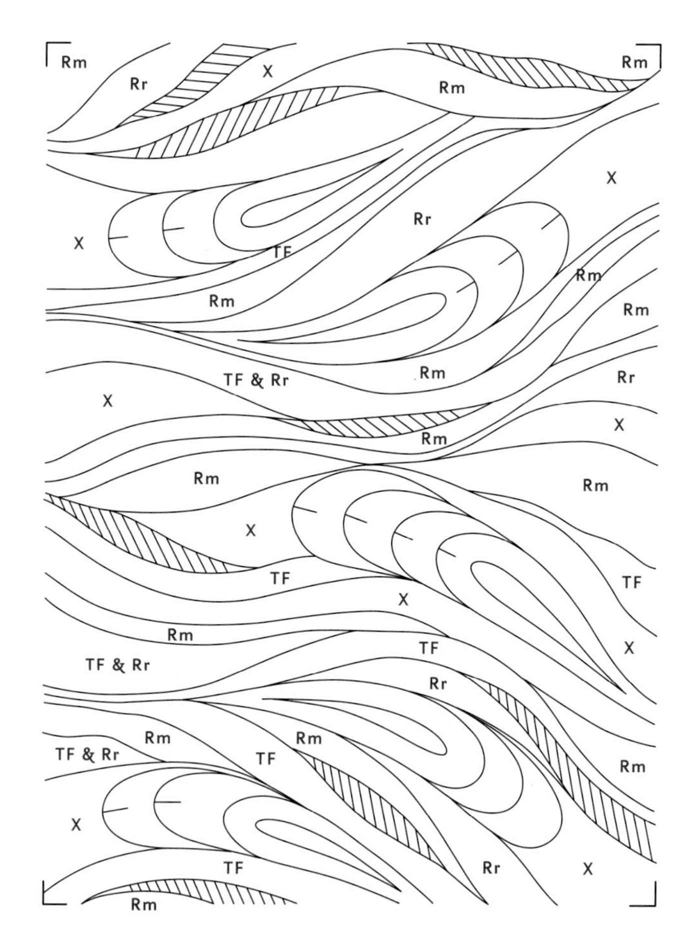

STITCHING CHART

TF = to and fro **Rr** = round and round
Rm = scatter effect with 3-cut beads **X** = scatter effect with bugle beads

Stitched by Christine Funnell of Tasmania, this bag uses the same techniques as PURPLE IRIS

9 Fitting the bag lining:

a) With the wrong side outermost, place the lining into the bag and check for fit. It should fit snugly except for the upper edge. Trim this edge to 7mm (5/16") above the lower edge of the metal frame.

b) Remove the lining and apply multi-use glue into the slot of the frame and spread it evenly it with a tooth pick.

c) Spread a very thin layer of PVA glue to the base of the wrong side of the lining.

d) Carefully fit the lining back into the bag and press the base to the base of the beaded piece. The glue will adhere the two pieces and prevent movement when used. If preferred, this part may be omitted.

e) Carefully fit the upper edge of the lining into the frame. Use a flat thin instrument (a cake decorating palette knife is good) and push the raw edges into the slot.

f) Fold in the seam allowance at the upper edge of the bag and lining sides. The two pieces should match up. Slip stitch the edges together.

It is preferable to leave the bag overnight for the glue to fully set before use. Because of the firm interfacing, there is no need to further steam and shape the bag.

HANAMI

Hanami is the traditional Japanese custom of welcoming spring; gathering under blooming Sakuras (cherry blossoms) to enjoy refreshments, friendship, song and the beauty of flowers. This project features a single Sakura flower as the focal point. The Sakura flower is synonymous with Japan and this design is a recognisable stylisation of this flower in Japanese society.

Techniques Used

Single stitches with one bead

Raised effect with general padding

Line of held thread

Line of held thread–circle method

Line of held thread–curved lines

Line of held thread–straight lines

Couching technique 1–combination needle-koma method

Vertical single layer

Separated single layer

Scatter effect technique –singles

Learning Points

Planning the embroidery sequence to achieve the best visual aesthetics

Using the ***couching technique 1–combination needle-koma method*** to create a circle and achieving a smooth line

Couching with ***couching technique 1–combination needle-koma method***

Using the ***line of held thread technique for straight lines***

Creating dimension
- ***raised effect with padding***
- tapering a flower through variation of colour and bead size

Achieving clean points

Achieving dimension with spacing

Creating a geometric lattice pattern

Fabric and Supplies

26cm (10 1/8") square of dark red quilting cotton

12cm x 18cm wide (4 3/4" x 7 1/8") piece of fusible medium wadding

Rectangular wooden box with an 11cm x 15cm wide (4 3/8" x 6") opening

Beads

Bead quantities listed refer to a 5cm x 12mm (2" x 1/2") tube

TOHO SIZE 11 SEED BEADS
A = 5CF transparent frosted ruby (2/3)
B = 87 transparent rainbow cobalt (1/4)
C = 119 transparent olivine lustre (1/4)
D = 163B transparent rainbow dk aqua (5 beads)
E = 241 rainbow lt topaz/mauve-lined (1/8)
F = 284 metallic green-lined aqua (1/4)
G = 506 teal blue iris higher metallic (1/4)
H = 779 rainbow crystal/salmon lined (1/8)

TOHO SIZE 15 SEED BEADS
I = 1 clear transparent (1/8)
J = 22 silver-lined lt gold (1/4)
K = 87 transparent rainbow cobalt (1/8)
L = 241 rainbow lt topaz/mauve-lined (1/8)
M = 284 metallic green-lined aqua (1/3)
N = 506 teal blue iris higher metallic (1/3)
O = 779 rainbow crystal/salmon-lined (1/8)

TOHO SIZE 12 2-CUT BEADS
P = 22 silver-lined lt gold (1/8)

TOHO SIZE 12 3-CUT BEADS
Q = 123 opaque lustre lt beige (1/2)

TOHO 3MM BUGLE BEADS
R = 22 silver-lined lt gold (2/3)

DESIGN AND PATTERN PREPARATION

Before any embroidery can commence the fabric must be prepared and framed up. Generally this proceeds in the following sequence:

1 Transfer the design to the fabric.

2 Frame up fabric.

3 Place pattern template over the design and outline using ***line of held thread technique.***

The design is rectangular in shape and measures 11cm x 15.3cm wide (4 3/8" x 6"). The corners are marked on the design. Use these as a guide to mark out the project or adjust as necessary to fit your box top.design and pattern preparation.

ORDER OF WORK

Sakura Flower

Centre

1 Stitch the centre as a small, five-petal flower using **Q** for the centre bead and **D** for the petals.

2 Stitch the stamens using **J** and the ***line of held thread technique.*** Tie down with one stitch at the midpoint. Begin with the stitches in the north-south direction. Work from the outer edge towards the centre with the stitch placement aimed at the midpoint of the centre bead.

3 Work stitches in the same manner in an east-west direction.

4 Add stitches in a NE, SW, NW and SE direction between the stitches worked.

5 Complete the stamen section by adding further stitches in the remaining spaces and ensuring that the circle shape is maintained.

Petals

1 Using **H** begin with the full foreground petals paying attention to the points and corners. Use the ***line of held thread technique*** for the short lines and ***couching technique 1–combination needle-koma method*** for the longer side lines.

2 Complete the background petals in a similar manner with the same beads.

3 Stitch two or three stamen lines in each petal using **E** tapering with **L** towards the centre. Where there are three stamen lines, stitch the centre line first then work a stitch on each side. Where there are only two lines, stitch the longer line first.

4 Fill in the petals with ***scatter effect-technique 1–singles*** using **H** and **O**. The smaller beads are used towards the centre and at the petal tips to create a tapering effect.

Stem

Stitch the stem using ***couching technique 1–combination needle-koma method*** using **C**.

Blue flowers

Centre

1 Begin with a single bead using **Q**. This stitch can be made in any direction.

2 Stitch a circle of beads around the centre using the ***line of held thread–circle method*** with **J**.

Petals

1 Pad the petals with stitches across the shape using **I**. Leave a one bead space around the edges and taper towards the centre of the flower by increasing the spacing (refer to the padding section for MAGENTA STAR).

2 Complete the surface embroidery for the petals using the ***vertical single layer technique.*** Begin with a stitch down the centre of the petal beginning with one **K**, then **B** and tapering to **J** for the last three to four beads. This stitch will not abut the flower centre. Re-enter the fabric 0.5mm (1/64") from the edge of the centre to create a ***one point space*** between the petals and the flower centre. Work the remaining stitches with **K** and **B** with the smaller beads placed on both ends of the stitch. Use the rounding principle for stitch placement to achieve a highly tapered shape at both ends of the petals (see ***weft layer*** and ***vertical layer*** techniques, page 36).

Leaves and stems

The order of stitching will depend on the position of the motifs. Always stitch the foreground motifs first, e.g. where a leaf joins to the side of a stem, the stem must be stitched first. Where the stem goes under a leaf at one end and another leaf or flower at the other end the stem is stitched last.

1 Stems: All stems are stitched using the ***couching technique 1–combination needle-koma method*** and **C**.

2 Leaves: Larger leaves are stitched using the ***separated single layer technique.***

a) Commence with a line of beads stitched using ***couching technique 1–combination needle-koma method.*** Couch between every bead. This represents the centre vein line.

b) Work diagonal stitches down one side of the leaf. It is preferable to start with the larger side of the leaf. Work these stitches from the tip down. Pay attention to the curve of the leaf and adjust the placement of the stitches to complement it. Stitches are worked from the outer edge in towards the center vein. Pin stitch in line.

c) Complete the remaining side in a similar fashion.

d) Where required, work tie-down stitches to complete the final shaping for the leaf.

Various bead combinations are used to stitch the leaves to create dimension, texture and flow. The combinations are given opposite. **J** is used for the centre line to represent the leaf vein and stem. Where size 15 and 11 beads are used, size 15 are only used at the beginning and end of each stitch for a tapering effect. The number of these smaller beads used will be dependent on the shape and curve of the leaf. Sometimes the last stitch at the base of the leaf may also use the smaller bead for shaping.

Combination 1: **G**, **N** and **J** (larger leaves)

Combination 2: **N** and **J** (smaller leaves)

Combination 3: **M** and **J** (smaller leaves)

Combination 4: **M**, **F** and **J** (larger leaves)

Lattice Background

1 With a fine pencil or white chalk pencil, draw two opposing sets of lines at 45 degrees to the base of the design. These lines will intersect at 90 degrees. To secure the best reference for stitching, choose a spot that will give a longer reference line.

2 These two lines are stitched first using the ***line of held thread–straight lines technique.*** **R** and **Q** beads are loaded alternately onto the thread. Couch between every bead on these two lines.

Subsequent stitches will be of one bead at a time building on the lattice pattern. Accurate stitch placement is key to this. As far as possible, stitch direction should be towards an existing bead.

Note: Even though it is possible to use longer stitches the single stitch will provide more stability for maintaining the lattice pattern.

3 At some point, along the edges, the space will not be sufficient to accommodate a bugle bead. In these instances, use **P** or **J** to fill.

Background

The remaining background is completed with ***scatter effect technique 1–singles*** using **A**. Frosted beads are used to allow the lattice and the Sakura flower to stand out.

CONSTRUCTION

Complete the finishing process

Construction is the same as CIRCLES. A larger seam allowance of at least 5cm (2") is recommended.

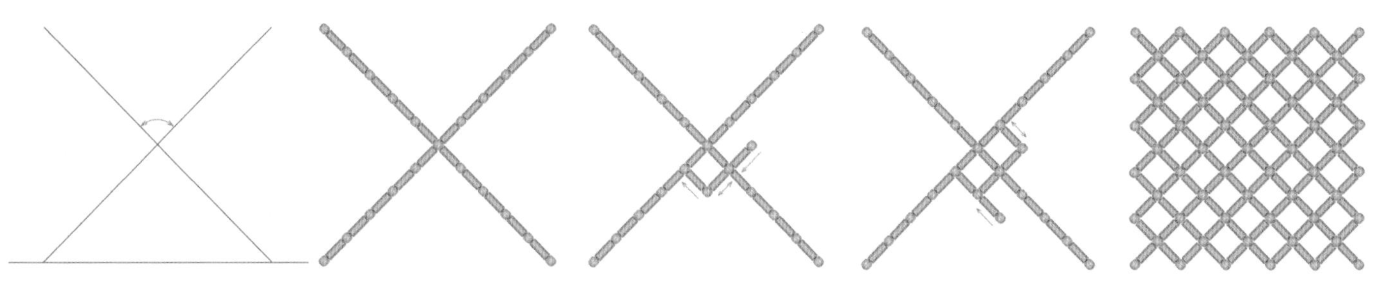

lattice background

WEDDING BELLS

This is a project for that special day and a keepsake for after. This design was adapted from a traditional silk-embroidered obi. A heart with the initials of the happy couple was added to the centre of the design with lines flowing inwards signifying the different attributes that each has brought to the unity. This project features both silk and bead embroidery and showcases the versatility of the art.

Techniques Used

Thread

Realistic random long and short stitch

Diagonal single layer

Fuzzy effect–vertically held lines

Line of staggered diagonals–4 step method

Beads

Vertical single layer

Diagonal single layer

Separated single layer

Line of held thread

Stamen effect

Couching technique 1–combined needle-koma method

Couching technique 2–long straight lines

Couching technique 4–round and round

Raised effect–padding and stitch length adjustment

Padding–general padding

Scatter effect technique 1–singles or doubles

Learning Points

Planning the embroidery sequence to achieve the best visual aesthetics

Using the ***couching technique 1–combination needle-koma method*** to create a circle and smooth line

Couching with komas

Creating dimension with
a) ***Raised effect by adjusting stitch length***
b) ***Raised effect with padding***
c) Tapering a flower by variation of bead colour and size

Achieving neat points

Fabric and Supplies

2 pieces 35cm x 30cm wide (14" x 12") ivory super smooth silk dupion

7cm x 100cm wide (2 3/4" x 40") strip of ivory super smooth silk dupion

30cm x 25cm wide (12" x 10") piece of fusible medium wadding

2m x 2mm wide (2yd8" x 1/16") ivory satin ribbon

30cm (12") ivory invisible zip

32cm x 2.5cm wide (12 1/2" x 1") white elastic

Silk sewing thread

Cushion insert

Beads and Threads

Bead quantities listed refer to a 5cm x 12mm (2" x 1/2") tube

TOHO SIZE 11 SEED BEADS
A = 21F silver-lined frosted crystal (1/4)
B = 161 transparent rainbow crystal (3)
C = 172 transparent rainbow pale green (1/2)

TOHO SIZE 15 SEED BEADS
D = 1 clear transparent (1/4)
E = 2 transparent lt topaz (1/3)
F = 21 silver-lined crystal (1/2)
G = 21F silver-lined frosted crystal (1/3)
H = 161 transparent rainbow crystal (1/3)
I = 172 transparent rainbow pale green (1/3)

TOHO SIZE 12 3-CUT BEADS
J = 101 transparent lustre crystal (3)
K = 161 transparent rainbow crystal (2)

TOHO SIZE 15 3-CUT BEADS
L = 101 transparent lustre crystal (1/3)

TOHO SIZE 12 HEXAGON BEADS
M = 161 transparent rainbow crystal (3/4)

SWAROVSKI BICONE CRYSTALS
N = 3mm crystal (5 pieces)
O = 4mm crystal unfoiled xilion (4 pieces)
P = 4mm jonquil (1 piece)

SWAROVSKI MARGUERITE CRYSTALS
Q = 6mm crystal foiled AB (4 pieces)
R = 6mm crystal unfoiled AB (4 pieces)

SWAROVSKI ROUND CRYSTALS
S = 4mm lt grey opeal (3 pieces)

SWAROVSKI XIRIUS LOCHROSEN CRYSTALS
T = 4mm crystal unfoiled AB (4 pieces)

SIZE 1 JAPANESE METALLIC THREAD
U = silver
V = lt gold
W = silver rainbow
X = II real laquer with sunago

FLAT SILK
Y = white

DESIGN AND PATTERN PREPARATION

Before any embroidery can commence the fabric must be prepared and framed up. Generally this proceeds in the following sequence:

1 Transfer the design to the fabric.

2 Frame up fabric

3 Place pattern template over the design and outline using ***line of held thread technique***.

The design is a 24cm x 29.5cm wide (9½" x 11⅝") rectangle. Position and transfer the design to the fabric.

Mark the outline of the cushion with a ***line of held thread*** and mark a second line 1cm (⅜") in from the outline in the same manner.

ORDER OF WORK

Metal thread and silk embroidery

Right diagonal stitches are worked in a clockwise direction along the motif and left diagonal stitches are worked in a counter-clockwise direction. Where a curve changes direction, identify the correct direction appropriate for the orientation and commence stitching to ensure that stitching progresses in the correct direction.

Inner heart shape

1 Using **V** and beginning at the tip, stitch the right side using the ***diagonal single layer technique***, with stitches oriented in a right diagonal direction.

2 Work the remaining side in a similar manner with the stitches oriented in a left diagonal direction.

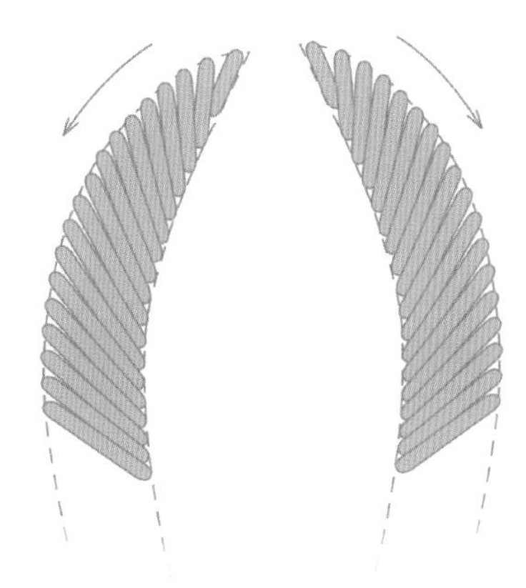

diagonal single layer: left and right

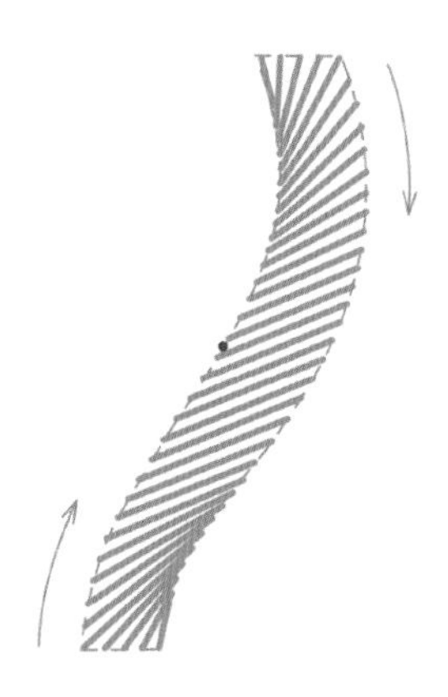

changing direction

Leaves 1: solid leaves

These leaves are stitched with the ***diagonal single layer technique*** in a right or left diagonal orientation as indicated on the stitching guide using **U**.

Leaves 2: Outlined leaves with fuzzy effect

1 Using **U** and **X**, work lines aligned with the weft direction of the fabric, spaced equally about 1mm (1/32") apart.

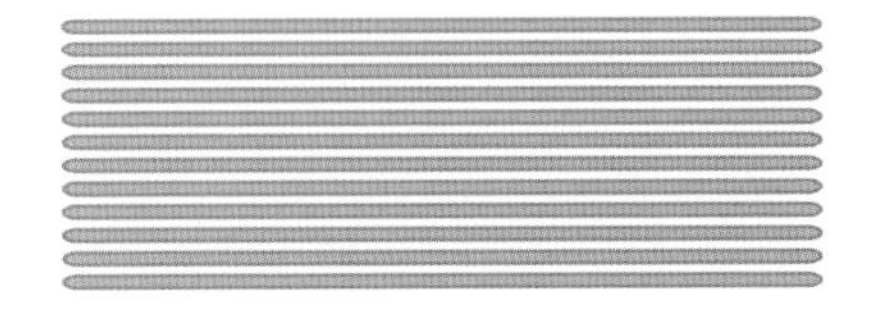

2 Tie these lines down with holding stitches about 2.5mm (3/32") apart using the same thread. Work one line at a time and offset with the holding stitches of adjacent lines.

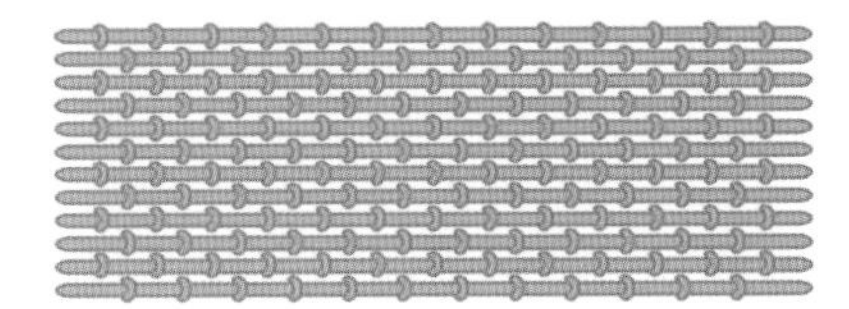

3 Outline the leaves with either one of two methods using **U**.

a) Outline with ***separated single layer*** using right diagonal on the right side and left diagonal on the left side. These leaves are labelled LR on the stitching guide. They should hide the ends of the fuzzy lines and will overlap them slightly.

b) Outline with ***line of staggered diagonals –4-step method.*** This technique is stitched as follows:

1 Begin with a stitch 1/3 the desired stitch length.

2 Work a second stitch starting to the immediate right of the first at the same level. This stitch is 2/3 the desired length.

3 Work a third stitch beginning to the immediate right of the second stitch at the same level as before. This is a full stitch length.

4 The fourth stitch is a full stitch length and begins level with the base of the first stitch.

5 Continue working full stepped stitches stepping down 1/3 space each time.

6 Finish with a 2/3 length and 1/3 stitch length.

7 If tapering is required omit steps 1 and 2 or step 6 as appropriate.

Rosebud

The rosebuds are completed in two sections.

1 The petal turnovers are stitched with the ***diagonal layer technique*** using **U**.

Stitch direction is indicated on the stitching guide.

2 The remainder of each bud is worked with ***realistic random long and short technique*** using **U** and **Y**.

a) Draw in contour lines for the individual petals.

b) Where motifs overlap, ensure a one point needle space is maintained between the motifs.

c) Begin with a row of ***long and short stitches*** using **U**. Begin with a stitch at the midpoint of the motif. Work first one side then the other. The stitches should be 5mm–9mm (3/16" x 3/8") in length. The contour line will determine the stitch length as the stitches must follow the direction of the contour lines.

d) When working the subsequent rows, take the needle up or down between the stitches following the contour lines. Again begin at the midpoint of the motif and stitches must follow the contour lines. Change to **Y** and continue with this thread until the motif is completed.

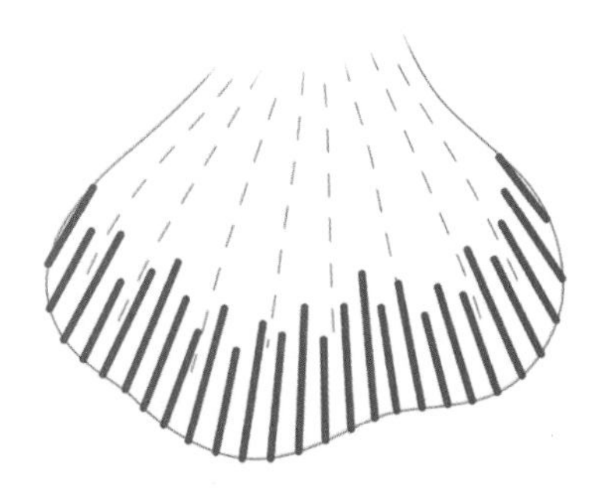

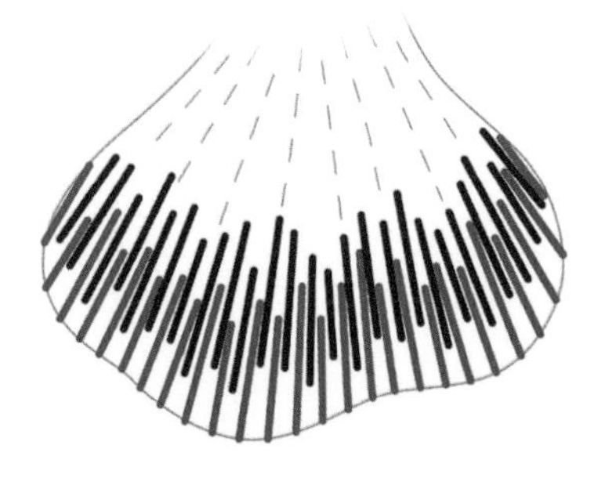

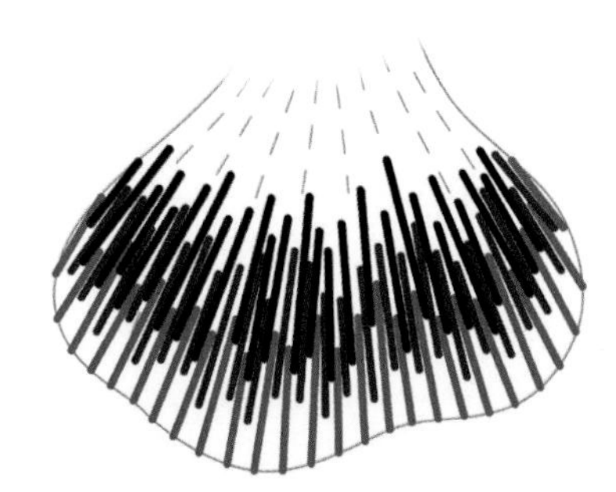

realistic randon long and short technique

Flower Bud

This bud is worked with silk and bead embroidery. Complete the two side petals with right diagonal stitches for the right side and left diagonal stitches for the left using **U**. Begin at the tip for both sides. Work the inner section with a line of **J** stitched with the ***line of held thread technique*** down the centre. Complete by adding single beads on either side of the line.

Inward flowing lines

This element is worked after all other bead motifs using **W**. These lines are worked using ***staggered diagonal technique–four-step method***. Work so that the stitching progresses in a clockwise direction for best results.

Where the line abuts another motif, irrespective of whether it is silk or beads, leave a single point space between the motifs.

Bead Embroidery

Cushion Outline

1 Using **K** work the two outlines using ***couching technique 2 – long straight lines***. Begin and turn corners with ***couching technique 4 - round and round***.

2 Using the same beads, work zigzag lines at approximately 45 degree angles between the two outlines. Triangles are formed when these lines are stitched.

3 Within each of these triangles, work three stitches using **M**. Make a vertical stitch with two beads aligned to the tip of the triangle and abutting the base.

4 Add a single stitch using the same beads on each side with the beads at a 45 degree angle against the bead at the base of the triangle.

Five-petal flowers

Pad the petals with stitches across the shape using **D**. Leave a one bead space around the edges and taper towards the centre of the flower by increasing the spacing. Complete the surface embroidery for the petals using the ***vertical single layer technique***. Begin with a stitch down the centre of the petal. Use the rounding principle for stitch placement to achieve a highly tapered shape at both ends of the petals.

1 Stitch the flowers using the following combinations for the petals:
G and **A**
L, **J** and **F**
H and **B**

2 The flower centres are stitched with a variety of *Swarovski* crystals using the ***stamen effect technique***. Where the flower centres are stitched with more than one crystal, use a random mix of finishes and types to fill the centre.

3 The recommended bead at the end of the stamen effect stitch is **L** but any of the other size 15 or 3-cut beads in the clear crystal colour range may be used.

Side view flower

1 Using ***couching technique 1–combination needle-koma method***, outline the two side lines with **G**.

2 Stitch diagonal stitches abutting the lines of (1) above using ***diagonal single layer technique*** using **G**.

3 Outline the curved sections using **F** and the ***line of held thread technique***. Work one section at a time and pay attention to achieving neat inward points with accurate stitch placement.

4 Stitch the three inner lines beginning with the centre stitch using **A** on the outer and tapering with **G** and **F** towards the centre.

5 Complete with ***scatter effect technique 2–singles and doubles*** using **L**.

Leaves

FULL LEAVES

These are stitched in the same way as the leaves in FLORAL PARADE, using **I**, **C** and **F**.

TYPE 1: HALF LEAVES

1 These are stitched with the ***diagonal single layer technique*** using **L** or a combination of **I** and **B**.

2 Begin stitching from the tip of the leaf. If the leaf curves counter-clockwise, use a left diagonal. If it curves clockwise, use a right diagonal.

Tendrils and stems

These are worked using ***couching technique 1–combination needle-koma method*** using **F**.

Background

1 Complete the background with ***scatter effect technique 1-doubles*** using **J**.

2 The background for the heart is worked with ***scatter effect technique 1– singles*** using **E**.

Ribbon Ties

Make the ribbon ties with the satin ribbon and sew to the top corners of the cushion.

CONSTRUCTION

1 ***Complete the finishing process.*** Fusible thin wadding may be added but this is optional. Cut out with a 1cm (3/8") seam allowance from the edge of the beading.

2 Cut the second piece of fabric in half crosswise and insert the zip. Trim the fabric until it is the same size as the front beaded piece.

3 Make a fabric tube three times the crosswise width of the project about 2.5–3cm wide (1"–1 3/16").

Cut the elastic the same length as the crosswise width of the project and insert into the tube. Ruche the fabric till the ends of the elastic and fabric tube line up.

Machine stitch through the ends to secure.

Note: Instead of using a sewing machine the cushion can also be assembled by hand, in which case seam together with small even back stitches.

4 Fit the band over the invisible zip and machine stitch in place.

5 With right sides together and matching raw edges pin the front and back together around the outer edge. Using a zipper foot, stitch around the edges.

6 Turn to the right side. Finger press the seams and corners to shape.

7 Place the cushion insert inside the cover and zip up.

Py

PAISLEY PARTY

Incorporating different paisley shapes, this project provides good practice for more challenging designs involving curves. The embroidery instructions and bead/ thread list are given for the glasses case only but the design is easily adapted to the evening bag. The pattern and construction details are provided for the evening bag and bead quantities should be doubled for this project. The evening bag was stitched by Dianne Conomos from Wentworth, NSW and uses some variation in bead choice.

This design is the last project in this book as judgment calls are required as stitching progresses because of the many overlapping elements. Choice of bead size and quantity will need to be made as these will differ according to variances in individual stitching. Prompts and hints are included in the instructions to assist in this process.

Techniques Used

Bead

Alternate vertical-horizontal line technique

Couching technique 1–combination needle-koma method

Line of held thread technique

Line of held thread–circle method

Raised effect–adjusting stitch length

Scatter effect technique 1–singles

Scatter effect technique 3–solid

Single stitches with one bead

Vertical single layer

Thread

Staggered diagonals–3-step method

Lattice grid

Learning Points

Planning the embroidery sequence to achieve the best visual aesthetics

Using ***couching technique 1–combination needle-koma method*** for different curves

Working abutting lines of beads

Creating decorative edges

Fabric and supplies

Glasses Case

23cm (9") square of cream silk taffeta

23cm (9") square of cream velvet

20cm (8") square of fusible thin wadding

20cm x 40cm (8" x 16") piece of fusible medium interfacing

PVA glue

White sewing thread

Evening Bag

50cm x 27cm wide (20" x 10½") piece of cream silk taffeta

44cm x 25cm wide (17½" x 10") piece of cream silk lining.

22cm x 44cm wide (8½" x 17½") piece of fusible thin wadding

22cm x 44cm wide (8½" x 17½") piece of fusible interfacing

22cm (8½") square of heavy interfacing

40cm (16") chain handle or braid

1 large or 2 small magnetic studs (optional)

PVA glue

Fabric adhesive

White sewing thread

Beads and threads

Bead quantities listed refer to a 5cm x 12mm (2" x ½") tube

TOHO SIZE 11 SEED BEADS
A = 1 clear transparent (1)
B = 2B medium topaz (1¼)
C = 5B Siam ruby (⅛)
D = 22 silver-lined light gold (1¼)
E = 34 silver-lined smoky topaz (⅓)
F = 147 transparent Ceylon cream (1½)
G = 148 Ceylon peach cobbler (1)

PRECIOSA SIZE 11 SEED BEADS
H = 57430 silver-lined lt green (1)

TOHO SIZE 15 SEED BEADS
I = 22 silver-lined lt gold (⅓)
J = 34 silver-lined smoky topaz (¼)
K = 162B medium topaz rainbow (⅓)
L = 558 permanent finish silver metallic (⅓)

TOHO SIZE 11 HEXAGON BEADS
M = 22 silver-lined lt gold (⅔)

TOHO SIZE 12 3-CUT BEADS
N = 141 Ceylon snowflake (1½)

TOHO SIZE 15 3-CUT BEADS
O = 83 metallic iris brown (⅓)

SIZE 1 JAPANESE METALLIC THREAD
P = lt gold
Q = bronze

DESIGN AND PATTERN PREPARATION

Before any embroidery can commence the fabric must be prepared and framed up. Generally this proceeds in the following sequence:

1 Transfer the design to the fabric.
2 Frame up fabric.
3 Place pattern template over the design and outline using ***line of held thread technique*** for straight lines and Japanese running stitch for curves.

Patterns for the glasses case and evening bag are provided.

ORDER OF WORK

Every attempt is made to follow the order of work in the instructions for the individual motifs but this is not entirely possible as some of the same design motifs may have to be worked later if they are overlapped by other foreground motifs.

The principle that the foreground motif must be stitched first must be adhered to.

Outline

1 Using **N** work the pattern outline using the ***alternate vertical-horizontal line technique***. The line of beads lies on the outside of the pattern template line

Paisley Shape 1

a) Begin with the large seven petal flower and stitch an **F** bead in the center. Encircle this with **L** using the ***line of held thread–circle method***.

b) Work each petal with two lines with the ***line of held thread technique*** using **D** and **I** tapering each end with the small beads and ensuring that neat points are achieved. Tie down the stitches to shape.

c) Work the star-shaped flowers using **F** for the centre and **D** for the petals. If necessary, add **I** to taper the petals towards the centre.

d) Outline the paisley shape with **H** using ***couching technique 1–combination needle-koma method***.

e) In the short sections between the star-shaped flowers, the ***line of held thread technique*** is used.

f) Work a second outline inside the first using **B**.

g) Using **P** and half-hitching the thread to the needle, stitch a ***line of staggered diagonals–3-step method*** inside the previous line of beads and a second line outside the first line of beads (**H**).

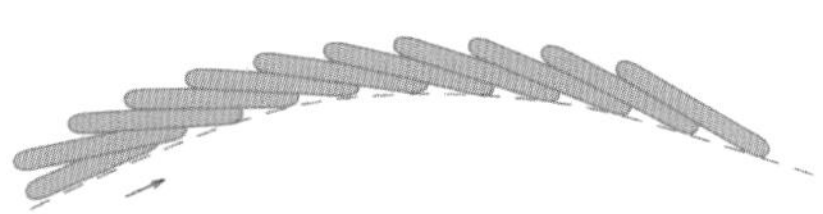

line of staggered diagonals–3-step

Inner paisley design

i Begin with the two small paisley shapes with ***couching technique 1–combination needle-koma method*** using **O**.

ii Work a 45 degree lattice grid, spaced 3mm (1/8") apart, using a single strand of **P** half hitched.

Lattice lines

- When working the lattice lines begin with a line worked at a 45 degree angle to the base of the design
- Work parallel lines at 3mm (1/8"), 4mm (3/32") or 5mm (3/16") intervals. 3mm (1/8") is used for the smallest paisley shapes and 5mm (3/16") for the large paisley shapes.

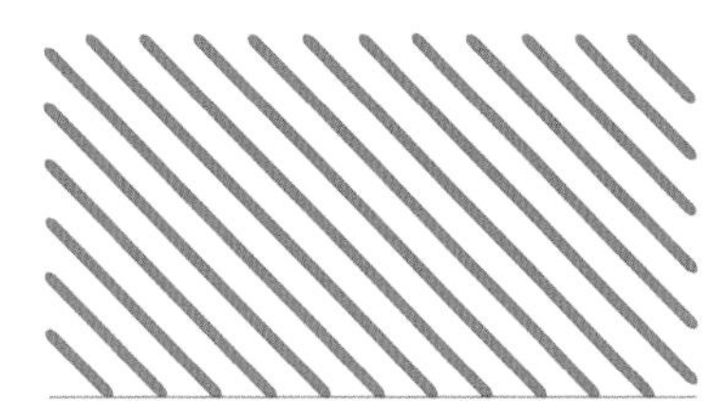

- Work a second set of parallel lines at the same intervals at 45 degrees in the opposite direction. The two sets of lines intersect at 90 degrees.

- Tie down threads at the intersections with a small horizontal or vertical stitch. All tie-down stitches should be worked in the same direction within a shape. Work the tie-down stitches in an orderly fashion working sequentially down each row of intersections until they are all tied down.

iii Stitch the arch between the paisley shapes with a line worked with ***line of held thread technique*** using **H**.

iv Work the two sprays of radiating stitches, using **L** and the ***line of held thread technique***. Tie down the stitches. Start with the centre stitch and complete one side and then the other. Tie down the stitches.

v Work small five-petals flowers using **F** for the center and **E** or **J** for the petals. They may also be stitched as six-petal flowers if desired. Correct placement and some small adjustment are required to accommodate the six beads. When the space becomes too small to accommodate the full flower work single stitches using **E**. Taper with **J** if desired.

vi Fill the background with **A** using ***scatter effect 3–solid***.

Paisley Shape 1A

a) Outline the shape with **D** using ***couching technique 1– combination needle-koma method.***

b) Work a second outline on the inside of the first using **G**.

c) Using **Q** half-hitched work a ***line of staggered diagonals–3-step method*** inside the previous line.

d) Work the inner 'v' shape using **O**.

e) Fill the background with **B** using ***scatter effect 3–solid.***

Paisley Shape 2

1 Outline the paisley shape with **D** using ***couching technique 1– combination needle-koma method.***

2 Work a second outline inside the first using **G**.

3 Using **Q** half-hitched work a ***line of staggered diagonals–3-step method*** inside the previous line.

4 Stitch the inner and overlapping paisley shapes with **O**.

5 Work a lattice grid with 4mm (5/32") spacing using **P**, half hitched.

6 Work small, five-petal flowers along the length of the paisley shape using **F** for the centre and **E** or **J** for the petals. Use smaller beads for the smaller spaces. When the space becomes too small to accommodate the full flower work single stitches using **E** or **J**.

7 Complete with ***scatter effect technique 3–solid*** using **B**.

Paisley Shape 2A

1 Outline the edge of the paisley shape with **G** using ***couching technique 1– combination needle-koma method.***

2 Work a second outline on the inside of the first using **D**.

3 On the outer edge, work single stitches of two beads, **M** on the outside and **D** on the inside, following the angles indicated by the design lines.

4 Work small five-petal flowers along the length of the paisley shape using **F** for the centre and **E** for the petals. Use **J** for the petals where the space is smaller. When the space becomes too small to accommodate the full flower work single stitches using **E** or **J**.

5 Complete with ***scatter effect technique 3–solid*** using **B**.

Paisley Shape 2B

1 Using **O** outline the edge of the shape with ***line of held thread.*** Progressively work additional outlines on the inner edges using **D**, **G** and **O**.

2 On the outer edge work single stitches of **M** following the angles indicated by the design lines.

3 Using ***single stitches with one bead*** work a line of **N** along the centre.

Paisley Shape 3

1 Outline the paisley shape with **D** using ***couching technique 1–combination needle-koma method.***

2 Work a second outline inside the first using **G**.

3 Work a third outline inside the previous using **O**. These beads are applied singly perpendicular to the shape at the point of the stitch. The stitch direction is always towards the line of the second outline. While still producing a linear effect the change in direction of the beads gives the line a softer look.

4 Work a lattice grid of 4mm (5/32") spacing using **P**, half hitched. Couch each intersection with the same thread. Add a single **J** bead in the centre of each square.

Scallop Shape 4

1 Work the shapes at the points with ***vertical single layer technique*** (tapered version) using **D**. Taper if desired with **I**.

2 Stitch the scalloped lines with the ***line of held thread technique*** using **D**, tying down between every bead. Pay attention to securing neat corner points. **I** can be used to taper the points, if desired.

3 Work small five-petal flowers between the shapes using **F** for the centre and **E** or **J** for the petals.

4 Work the shape below Paisley shape 5 using the ***vertical single layer technique*** (tapered version) and add dimension by creating a slight raised effect by adjusting stitch length. Using **B**, begin with a stitch down the centre of the shape. Alternating from side to side, continue to work stitches using **K** to taper if desired.

Paisley Shape 5

1 Outline the paisley shapes with **H** using ***couching technique 1–combination needle-koma method.***

2 Work an outline encompassing the two paisley shapes with **B** using ***couching technique 1–combination needle-koma method.***

3 On the outside edge, work single stitches of two beads, **M** on the outside and **D** on the inside, following the angles indicated by the design lines.

4 Stitch small five-petal flowers using **F** for the centre and **E** or **J** for the petals.

5 Using **C** work the arch between the paisley shapes using the ***line of held thread technique.***

6 Work the spray of radiating stitches using **L** and the ***line of held thread technique.*** Tie down the stitches. Begin with the centre stitch, then complete one side then the other.

7 Work the two tiny cross shapes formed by two curved lines using **L** and the ***line of held thread technique.***

8 Stitch small five-petal flowers using **F** for the centre and **E** or **J** for the petals. Add 3–4 **L** beads tapering towards the tip.

9 Complete the paisley shapes with ***scatter effect technique 1–singles*** using **A**.

10 Complete the central heart shape with ***scatter effect technique 1–singles*** using **N**.

Paisley Shape 6

1 Outline the scalloped edge of the paisley shape using **O** with ***line of held thread technique–curved lines*** for the shorter lines and ***couching technique 1–combination needle-koma method*** for the longer lines and those with tight curves.

2 Outline the peaked dome using **G** with ***couching technique 1–combination needle-koma method.***

Note: Depending on how you have stitched the surrounding foreground shapes part of the outline of the shape may be obscured. If this is the case work only the visible part of the outline.

---

3 Stitch a second outline on the inside of the first using **O**.

4 Outline the inner paisley shape with **H** using ***couching technique 1–combination needle-koma method.*** Add single stitches spaced one bead apart between the edges using **J**. Work an outline on the outer edge of the shape using **O**.

5 Stitch the arch and flower spray in the same manner as Paisley shape 5 using **C** and **L**. Add a few single stitches using **N** between the spray if space allows.

6 Work small five-petal flowers using **F** for the centre and **J** for the petals.

7 Complete with ***scatter effect technique 3–solid*** using **A** between the five-petal flowers.

Paisley Shape 7

1 Outline the shape using **D** and the ***line of held thread technique.***

2 Stich a second outline on the inside of the first using **G**.

3 Stitch a third outline using **O**.

4 If space permits add a fourth line with **B** or a single bead in the remaining space available. Depending on the space **I** can be used.

Paisley Shape 8

1 Outline the shapes with **H** using ***couching technique 1–combination needle-koma method.***

2 Stitch small, five-petal flowers using **F** for the centre and **J** for the petals. When the space becomes too small to accommodate a full flower work single stitches using **L**.

3 Complete with ***scatter effect technique 3–solid*** using **A**.

Paisley Shape 8A

This is worked in the same way as Paisley Shape 8 except a second outline is added on the inside of the first using **B**.

Paisley Shape 9

1 Stitch a single **F** bead in the centre.

2 Work a line of beads in a semi-circle around the centre using **L** and the ***line of held thread technique.***

3 Work the remaining portion as if it was a flower using **B** and **I** or **K**. **I** and **K** are used towards the inner section for a tapered effect. Work the first two lines of beads to line up with the edge of the completed paisley shape or the edge of

the pattern (where applicable). These two lines can now be viewed as the north-south petal line of a symmetrical flower. Complete the shape by fitting petals in the spaces between.

Paisley Shape 10

1 Stitch the outline using **O** and the ***line of held thread technique.***

2 Work the three inner lines beginning with the centre line and using **L**. Tie down the lines.

Background

Complete the embroidery by filling the remaining background with ***scatter effect technique 2–singles and doubles*** using **N**.

Upper bag edge

The opening of the bag is outlined and a decorative stitch is created with some basic stitches.

a) Measure and mark a line 7mm (5/16") down from the upper edge of the bag.

b) Beginning from A work a diagonal stitch with 6–7 beads to B. Make a pin stitch.

c) Bring the needle to the front at C and work a diagonal stitch with 7–9 beads to D. This stitch overlaps the first line and requires more beads. Pin stitch.

d) Bring the needle to the front at B and make a diagonal stitch with 6–7 beads to E. Pin Stitch.

e) Bring the needle to the front at D and work a diagonal stitch with 7-9 beads to F. Pin stitch.

Continue in this pattern with cross lines alternating the overlapped stitches and bead colours.

f) Small triangles and diamonds will form. Add a bead at the centre of each space.

CONSTRUCTION

Glasses case

1 ***Complete the finishing process.***

2 With the work still on the frame, measure the beaded piece. Using the measurements cut out:

a) Fusible thin wadding–Trim away 2mm (1/16") from each long edge. Check against the beaded piece.

b) Fusible medium interfacing. Trim away 2mm (1/16") from each long edge. Check against the beaded piece.

Using the lining pattern piece cut out:

c) Fusible medium interfacing

d) Lining fabric with a 1cm (3/8") seam allowance. The weft of the fabric should be along the width of the pattern.

3 Fuse the wadding to the back of the beaded piece. Fuse the interfacing to the wadding. Allow to cool.

4 Remove the beaded piece from the frame and cut out with a 1cm (3/8") seam allowance. Clip the curved edges. Apply glue to the edge of the seam allowance only. Fold the seam allowance under and press in place.

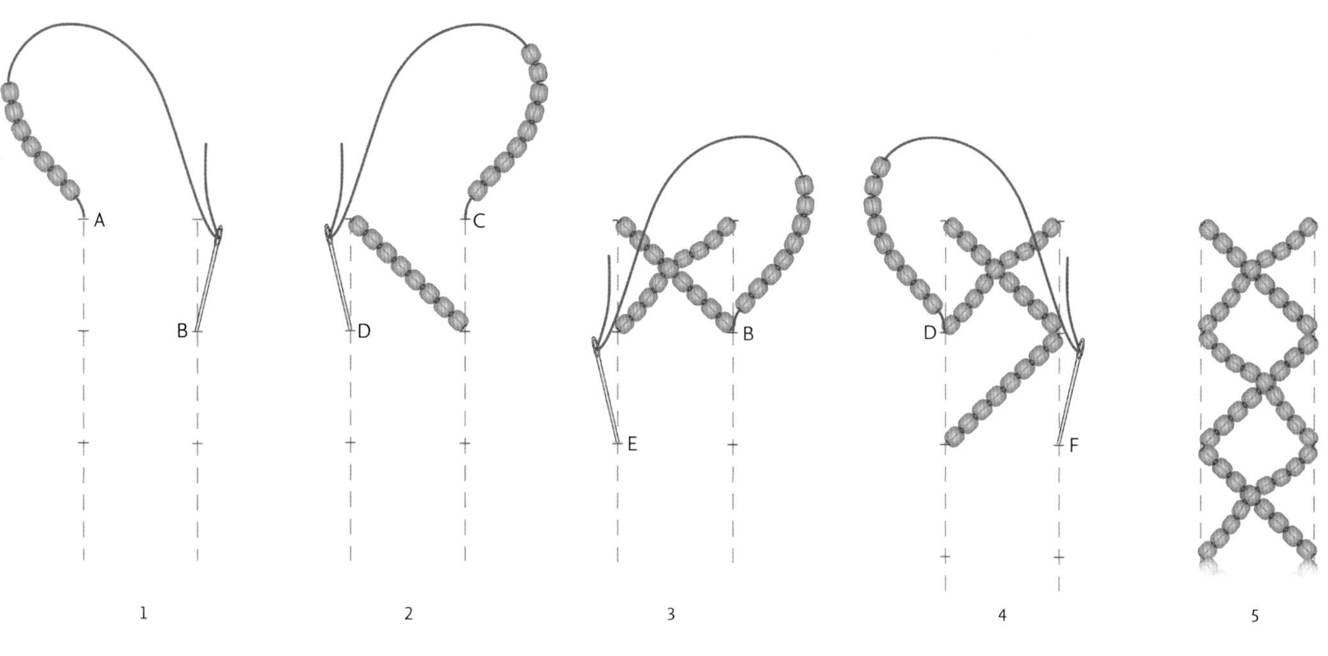

upper bag decorative edge

The folded edge should lie just under the line of beads.

Note: Do not allow the glue to touch the fabric along the folded edge as it will make subsequent stitching difficult.

---

5 Fuse the interfacing to the wrong side of the lining fabric. Fold under the seam allowance and glue or tack in place as before.

6 Attach the lining to the beaded piece making sure that the edges at the opening end line up. The lining should be slightly smaller than the beaded cover to allow for the fold. Fit the edges at the opening end of the beaded piece and lining together first. Beginning at the midpoint slipstitch the lining to the beaded piece along one side.

When complete return to the centre and repeat for the remaining side.

7 Fit the lining to the remaining three sides ensuring that there are no creases and slipstitch in place.

Note: Greater accuracy will be achieved if this is stitched with the pieces folded over. This is cumbersome but well worth the effort.

---

8 Fold the piece in half aligning the edges and stitch together with ladder stitch using a doubled thread.

Use a bulldog clip to hold the sides together while stitching. Begin at the base and finish at the opening. At the corner, reinforce the stitching for added strength. Ensure that the stitches are made just under the beaded edge as the beading should finish as close together as possible.

9 On completion, crumple acid-free tissue paper and place inside the case. Manipulate the tissue until the desired shape is achieved. Steam the piece with a wet cloth over a dry iron or a commercial steamer.

10 Remove the wet tissue and replace with fresh dry tissue. Check that the project is still in the desired shape. Reshape if necessary by manipulating the fresh tissue. Leave to dry overnight before use.

Evening Bag

1 ***Complete the finishing process.***

2 With the piece still on the frame, measure the beaded areas and check that the size remains true. Using the measurements, cut out :

a) Backing for the beaded pieces:

i Fusible thin wadding

ii Fusible interfacing

Cut both to an exact fit. Trim 1mm (1/32") off each long edge.

b) Fusible interfacing for the lining

c) Lining fabric with 1cm (3/8") seam allowance added. The weft of the fabric should be across the pattern.

3 Fuse the wadding then the interfacing to the back of the beaded pieces. Allow to cool.

4 When cool, remove the beaded pieces from the frame and cut out adding a 1cm (3/8") seam allowance.

5 Stitch the darts with ladder stitch.

6 Apply glue to the edge of the seam allowance only. Fold under the seam allowance and glue in place. The folded edge should lie just under the line of beads.

Note: Do not allow glue to touch the fabric along the folded edge as it will make subsequent stitching difficult.

---

a) Align and stitch the two parts together with ladder stitch using a double thread for strength. The stitches should catch the fabric directly under the beads. Begin at the midpoint at the base and work up one side. Return and complete the remaining side in the same way.

b) Use a bulldog clip to hold the sides together while stitching to keep the edges from slipping.

c) At the upper edges, double back on the stitches for added strength. Ensure that the stitches catch the fabric just under the beaded edge as the beaded edges should finish as close together as possible.

7 Fuse the interfacing to the lining fabric.

8 Stitch the darts in the lining fabric. With right sides together, stitch the lower edge and the sides. Stitch a second line close to the first. Trim the seam allowance to 1mm (1/32") from the outer stitch line and reinforce with fabric adhesive around the edges.

9 Fitting the beaded piece and lining together.

a) Trim the seam allowance on the upper edge to 5mm (3/16") above the bead line for the beaded piece and the interfacing for the lining. Fold under and tack in place.

b) Place the lining into the beaded piece and check for fit. Adjust if necessary.

c) Spread a very thin layer of glue to the base of the lining on the wrong side.

d) Place the lining back into the purse and press the base of the lining to the base of the beaded piece. The glue will hold the two pieces together and prevent movement when used. If preferred, this may be omitted.

e) If adding a purse chain or braided strap, sew the strap in place at this point.

f) Align the edges of the beaded piece and lining. Slipstitch the upper edges together.

g) Attach the magnetic studs to the upper edge of the bag lining if desired.

I have often been asked how one goes about translating design to bead embroidery. To this end I adopt a planning approach that has been instilled in me through my practice of Chinese art embroidery.

Included is a template that you might find useful for your own planning process.

Earlier in this book, commercially designed and printed fabric was identified as a ready design source for Japanese-style bead embroidery. The two case studies in this section will focus on this.

CASE STUDY

Celebration of Flowers

This fabric is from the *Kiev-Russian Florals* Range designed by Maureen McNaughton for *Elizabeth Studios*. It was one of those 'Bead Me' moments.

The design was not without its challenges but the process of translating it to bead embroidery was a real delight.

Planning template

To illustrate the use of this template, it is applied to Celebration of Flowers and a detailed analysis is made for the main flower only. While the same detailed analysis is not given for the other flower and design elements in Part 2 of the Case Study Guide, technique selection and comments along with any pertinent learning points are provided.

This case study was stitched by Elisabeth Steimetz of South Australia.

PLANNING TEMPLATE

Visual summary of design	
Proposed project and suitability of design	
Foreseeable challenges	

ANALYSIS OF OVERALL DESIGN

Component	Considerations
Elements	
Colour complexity	
Movement	
Dimensional perspective	

ANALYSIS OF ELEMENTS

Elements	Challenges presented	Solution	Technique and colour selection	Comments/reminders

CELEBRATION OF FLOWERS STITCHING GUIDE

E Innermost Petals

1 Foreground
- Vertical stitches
- Create ***raised effect–adjusting stitch length***

2 Background
- Vertical stitches
- Use red thread
- No raised effect

C Petal Turnover
- Diagonal stitches
- Begin from the tip

D Outer Petals

1 Foreground petals
- Pad outline
- ***Long and short technique***

2 Background petals
- Vertical stitches–start at the centre

H Outermost Petals
- Vertical stitches
- Create ***raised effect–adjusting stitch length***

B Small Green Bracts

1 Vertical stitches

2 Create ***raised effect–adjusting stitch length***

F Corolla Flower

1 Begin with ***single stitches with one bead*** for centre

2 Vertical stitches for each petal–create ***raised effect–adjusting stitch length***

G Corolla

1 Begin with the outline using ***line of held thread method***

2 Fill with ***long and short technique***

A Flower Centre

1 Begin with one single bead

2 Circle with ***line of held thread–circle method***

3 8 single crystal spaced equally

ANALYSIS DOCUMENT: CELEBRATION OF FLOWERS

Name of Project: CELEBRATION OF FLOWERS | **Print fabric:** *Kiev Russian Florals* by Maureen McNaughton for *Elizabeth Studios*

Visual summary of design	A variety of distinct bright flowers in a scrolling movement across the weft of the fabric with distinct border designs. The distinct orientation of the design is dictated by the largest flower.
Proposed project and suitability of design	Lends itself to decorating a box top with the largest flower as the focal point.
Foreseeable challenges	• Multiple component parts of similar colour within a single element, particularly the central flower. • Fine points and tight curves of design. • Projecting linear perspective suggested by the design

ANALYSIS OF OVERALL DESIGN

Component	Considerations
Elements	Three distinct flower types, two main types of leaves, tendrils and elements, symmetrical border pattern.
Colour complexity	Considered high: Gradual colour shading within small areas; small overlapping motif with similar colourings.
Movement	Large variety of curves involved including turnover sections. There is movement within individual elements as well as the overall design that must flow together.
Dimensional perspective	Definite dimensional perspective present and to be reflected especially for the flowers.

ANALYSIS OF ELEMENTS

Elements	Challenges presented	Solution	Technique and colour selection	Comments/reminders
Main flower	Flower petals turn and recede into the center - likely the most important consideration.	Create strong differential in perspective.	• ***Outline padding*** to increase prominence at the edges. • Realistic effect with vacant spacing and smaller beads towards centre to recede. • Bead colour to change from light to dark towards the centre to recede the centre.	Ensure good contour lines are maintained.
	Turnover of petals to be evident and distinct from remaining petals whilst maintaining similar colours.	Ensure visual separation.	Use different techniques and colour variation at the overlapped area to create the distinction.	***Diagonal single layer technique*** for turnover section and ***realistic effects –random long and short vertical*** for the main petal.

ANALYSIS OF ELEMENTS

Elements	Challenges presented	Solution	Technique and colour selection	Comments/reminders
	Similar small flowers at top of design and in the mid-section but perspective is different due to backward tilt of flower.	Increase the prominence of flowers in the mid-section and reduce the ones at the tip.	Use different techniques and bead sizes.	Use single crystal beads for each flower in the center and size 15 beads for the flowers on the top.
	Similar colour of overlapping petals.	Create variation without compromising colours.	• Beads at different angles in overlapped areas. • Use transparent beads and alter shading by using different colour threads.	Red thread for the back-ground petals alternating with the usual white thread for the other surrounding petals.
	Corolla of the flower emerges from the hidden centre section and must be reflected.	Recede the corolla and increase the prominence of the foreground overlapping motif.	• Increase prominence of the foreground petal with ***raised effect***. • Recede the corolla with negative space	Use smaller beads for the corolla.

This flower has three main components: the calyx, centre petal and side petals.

The sequence of stitching based on the 'foreground first' principle will be:

1 Centre petal
2 Calyx
3 Side petals

Centre petal

1 Begin with the foreground red spiral as this shape needs to be preserved. ***Couching technique 1–combination needle–koma method.***
2 Use ***vertical single layer*** for the petal. Begin with the lower part and commence with the centre stitch. Complete one side and then the other. Shorten stitches slightly to give a hint of ***raised effect*** to reflect the roundness of the petal.
3 Create a ***raised effect with general padding.*** General padding is used here to elevate the upper section more than the lower half and to taper it towards the base. Complete the surface stitching for the upper section beginning with the centre stitch – matching this stitch to the corresponding contour line in the lower section. Note that this is not necessarily the same centre line due to the curved shape of the petal.

Side petals The aim here is to represent curved petals receding behind the centre petal.

- ***Outline padding*** to raise the outer edge.
- Over stitch with ***long and short technique*** with darker and smaller beads toward the centre. The negative space of the ***long and short technique*** along with the smaller and darker beads will create a strong curved and receding visual effect.

Calyx – ***Line of held thread*** for the two side stitches then a centre stitch in a different colour for the vein. Ensure that neat points are achieved with good stitch placement.

In terms of perspective, this flower is further back than the two previous ones, so it needs to recede more.

1 Begin the flower centre using ***line of held thread–circle method.***

2 Stitch the main veins beginning from the tip with colour changing to gold using ***couching technique 1–combination needle-koma method***. This sets the line and flow for the flower petals.

3 Stitch the petals with ***separated single layer technique*** (right diagonal on right and left diagonal on left). An orange thread and clear beads are used.

- The orange thread maintains the colour theme and the clear beads mute the thread colour.
- The orange thread combined with the transparent orange beads result in a more subdued colour compared with the main flower, causing it to recede.

4 **Lower petal** – stitched in ***vertical single layer technique***. Colour is changed for the adjoining petal to separate them.

5 **Calyx** – ***line of held thread*** – 2 strands. Ensure neat points.

6 Fill in the blue central section with ***scatter effect***. The ***scatter effect*** produces colour with no defined lines.

This flower has no complicated requirements but working order is important to maintain the integrity of various shapes.

1 The first step is to set the foreground shape, which is partly delineated by the inner line of the flower centre. Outline this with gold beads using ***couching technique 1–combination needle-koma method***.

2 Stitch the centre section with diagonal stitches – create ***raised effect*** at the bulbous section following the design lines. The two outer-edge stitches are flat and will be tied down to support and maintain the shape of the two raised central stitches. Note that the stitch lines make up the outline for the remaining edge of the bud. Accurate stitch placement is crucial for this.

3 Fill in space with ***scatter effect*** using a dark colour to enhance the shape.

4 Stitch the side petals with the ***line of held thread technique***. Begin each with the two outside lines before filling in the centres with either one or two stitches.

5 Work the calyx with one centre bead enclosed with a line of beads stitched with the ***line of held thread technique***.

ALL LEAVES

Full Leaves:

1 Begin with the centre vein changing the colour of the beads where necessary.

2 Separated diagonal stitches. Right diagonal for right side and left diagonal for left side, working from the tip.

Half Leaves: Diagonal stitches (left or right diagonal as dictated by the orientation of the leaves).

Round Leaves: Vertical layer technique. Create ***raised effect*** near tip by ***adjusting stitch length***. Although it is a ***raised effect***, occasionally tie-down stitches are used discreetly towards the base to maintain the flow of the curve. Accurate stitch placement is paramount for these leaves to avoid too many tie-down stitches which can leave the finished product looking stiff.

All stems & tendrils: *Couching technique 1–combination needle-koma method.*

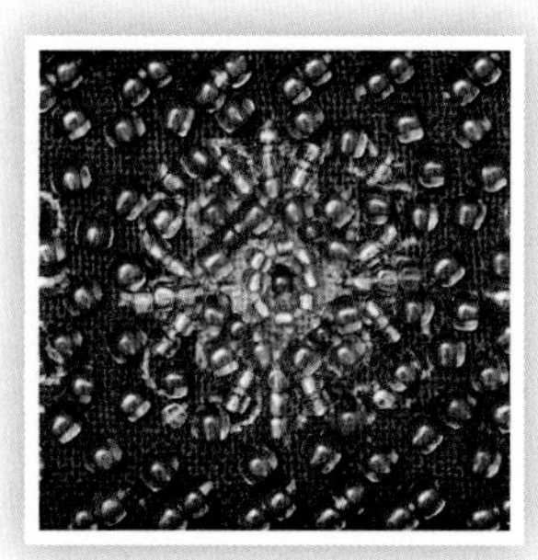

Outline: It was felt that a straight outline of beads was too harsh for the rambling nature of the design. To create a more relaxed appearance, diagonal stitches (two beads per stitch) set at an angle of about 45 degrees and spaced one bead apart are stitched.

Pattern within outline:

The design in itself is too small to follow exactly so was used as a guide to create a pattern that is similar.

1 Begin the centre with a single bead and surround with ***line of held thread –circle method***.

2 Stitch four side spokes – each made up of single vertical stitch and two side diagonal stitches.

3 Fill in with a single small bead surrounded with three single beads equally spaced. This makes up the inner corner.

4 Complete with a single bead placed to form an outer corner.

Background:

- Main background: completed with ***scatter effect technique 2–singles and doubles***. 3-cut opaque beads are used to add texture.
- Border: completed with ***scatter effect technique 1–singles*** with round beads. In contrast to the main background the round beads produce a more static effect.

CASE STUDY

Arabian Nights

Finding a suitable fabric to embellish is not always the easiest mission - at least for me it is not.

The common question that is often asked is: Do I look for fabric first and then decide on the project or should I look for any fabric that may look to have potential and then decide on the project?

To this, I often reply with another question. How often have you gone to the shops intending to buy an item and come away with something that is anything but - It is a bit like that in the search for fabric.

I have trained myself to deliberately keep 'project' out of my conscious mind and also any preconceived ideas for fabric designs. If you browse with an open mind the right fabric will speak to you and inspiration for the right project will also start to flow. Having said all that, a word of caution; not every pop up design is suitable as is. Be forewarned that you may have to contribute a bit of creative licence to make it work for bead embroidery. After all, fabrics are designed for a different purpose than for bead embroidery.

I came across the fabric for this case study quite by accident on one of my overseas teaching trips. Blue is not my colour but it was the design that attracted me. It reminded me of Arabic designs and architecture - hence the title Arabian Nights for the beaded version. Additionally, with a colour not being one that I normally work, I felt

that the challenge of being outside my comfort zone would help to develop me further in the craft. I have since added to my stash the same fabric design in my favourite warm red and yellow hues.

The fabric is from the *Kashmir* range designed by *Jinny Beyer*.

As with Celebration of Flowers an analysis will only be done for the main central shape to give a picture of how I approach a complicated design. Other interesting parts of the fabric design will be discussed from a stitching and technique point of view with commentary for pertinent learning points.

Let us now start the bead embroidery.

It is very natural to assume that stitching will commence with the centre heart which is the dominant shape. For this design, the centre heart and the scallop edge motif on each side are connected by lines which become part of the centre shape. This makes the centre heart shape background to the scallop edge motif, which should be stitched first... BUT WAIT... all the shapes work up to and abuts the straight edge of the lower striped border. Therefore this is the first thing to be done. The straight edge on the upper side does not have the same consideration so can be done later.

This edge is stitched with bugle beads spaced slightly apart to form a straight line.

As bugle beads are planned for the centre heart shape in the analysis stage, it is good to use them in other suitable areas to link the overall design together. Bugle beads are also used in other areas for this same reason.

ANALYSIS DOCUMENT: ARABIAN NIGHTS

Name of Project: ARABIAN NIGHTS | **Printed fabric:** *Kashmir* range by *Jinny Beyer*

Visual summary of design	A fabric comprising strips of pattern in different tones of the principal colour with highlights of black and brown. The strips alternate between a wide strip of 13.5cm (5 3/8"), comprising a mix of distinct shapes artfully combined, and a narrow strip of 5cm (2") with a repeating elongated pattern.
Proposed project and suitability of design	The main design is oriented in the weft on of the fabric and design symmetry is involved. Each strip is edged on both sides with a line of small repeating shapes.
Foreseeable challenges	The design presents many possibilities for a larger sized project including bags and purses, box top, book cover and cases for electronic products. • The multiple elements and limited colour scheme. • Fine points and tight curves of design. • Different shapes must be distinctive yet correlate.

ANALYSIS OF OVERALL DESIGN

Component	Considerations
Elements	• Three principal large shapes arranged in a symmetrical design within the main strip with one being the central and larger shape. • Minor shapes within the main shapes. • Shapes connecting the principal shapes. • Small repeating shapes of different pattern edging both strip.
Colour complexity	Only three main hues but different tones. Challenge lies in working with limited colours and multiple elements.
Movement	Movement is within the elements while symmetry is key to the overall design.
Dimensional perspective	No significant linear or dimensional perspective.

ANALYSIS OF ELEMENTS

Elements	Challenges presented	Solution	Technique and colour selection	Comments/reminders
Central heart design	This central shape has to be the standout part of the design. Challenge lies in achieving this while maintaining colour scheme.	The shape must standout with strong movement created that will draw the eye to it.	• Introduce a contrasting light colour outside the fabric hues to the centre of the main shape to create a visual focal point. • Create strong lines to draw the eye towards the focal point – technique choice for each part must be geared towards the solution. • ***Raised effect*** to give it more prominence.	Adjust bead sizes to taper and further draw the eye in.

Elements	Challenges presented	Solution	Technique and colour selection	Comments/reminders
Inner pattern of dark lines	Inner motif created by black lines – many curved ends involved.	Artistic licence - maintain the lines and simplify the ends. At the end of the curved arms, instead of finishing with the couched line, introduce a small five-petal flower which evokes the curved end without the problem identified. Five-petal flower also ties in with the design as it is a motif in the other shapes. The bonus with this solution will be that the centre bead in a different colour will emphasise the curve.	• 3-cut beads for the five-petal flower and line. Round beads will make the five petals show up as they are set in a different direction to the line. The 3-cut beads, by their nature will negate this. • Use two different shades of black beads for the two inner black lines. The slight difference will give individual perspective. • ***Line of held thread*** for short lines and ***couching technique 1–combination needle-koma method*** for the longer lines.	
Inner space formed by dark lines	Creating the inner focal point.	Create a point of highlight. Bead lines to draw the eye to this point.	• Beads in a strong contrasting colour are introduced - in this case, an iridescent white was selected. • Larger faceted round crystal bead is selected to create the focal point. • Small straight stitches fill the background pointing towards the centre of the crystal bead.	Use single crystal beads for each flower in the center and size 15 beads for the flowers on the top.
Background within the heart shape	The normal ***scatter effect*** will create a comparatively static space and break up the flow as the area is comparatively larger than all other background areas within the strip.	A pattern with clean lines that will complement the flow. Fabric pattern itself suggests a shape.	• Bugle beads will reduce texture with their longer lines. • Single stitches following the shape and distributed to create a flow. • Potential use of negative space for emphasis.	
Outer finlike shape surrounding the heart	Area is relatively wide. Its size has the potential to distract the eye from the centre, which has been stitched flat.	Create some dimensional perspective with the centre shape. Visually reduce the space.	• Lighter tone to be used than the other parts of the shape to retain emphasis toward the centre. • Shade of beads for the line abutting the dark lines must balance the dark beads and the colour of the outer shape. • Select two colours of beads to break up the width of the shape. • Outline padding to create dimensional perspective. The inward receding flow will draw attention back towards the centre.	Make use of smaller beads to taper and achieve neat points. Stitch placement is critical to creating flow for this shape. Pad and stitch each 'fin' section separately. At inward corners make a decision if padding is required. Stitching by sections makes this possible.

SCALLOPED SHAPE A

1 Stitch the outer scalloped lines with metallic bronze tapering with smaller beads at the points and ends. Use ***couching technique 1–needle-koma method*** as although the length is relatively short, the curves are very tight. The alternative ***line of held thread technique*** may not produce the same tension and even spacing.

2 Work the outer line in a similar manner following the previous line with the dark bead. The lines abut each other.

3 Stitch the feather shaped inner section. Work as ***separated single layer*** with two bead colours along each stitch. Smaller beads are used to help taper where required. Give a hint of ***raised effect***. Stitches must be spaced or they will crowd.

Note: Although the ***separated layer technique*** *is applied, the sequence of stitching has to be modified as the curve changes direction. This has particular stitch placement implications for the concave side. Stitching will be as follows to circumvent the potential problem:*

a) Make a stitch at the top midpoint of the feather shape.

b) Start the first stitch at point A and work down in left diagonal single layer till the end. Return to point A and work in left diagonal up to the first stitch of (a). Be aware that stitches should present continuity so make sure that stitch placements are accurate to achieve this.

c) Continue down the other side in a right diagonal single layer.

---

4 Stitch the inner separation line with ***single beads*** tapering with smaller beads and increased spacing towards the base.

5 Stitch five-petal flowers with metallic bronze for the centre and silver for the petals This continues to bring in the contrasting colour as planned into the overall design in a discreet and harmonious way.

6 Complete the designs with diagonal lines using metallic bronze in ***line of held thread method***.

CENTRAL HEART SHAPE

1 Begin with the scalloped lines using ***couching technique 1–needle-koma method*** using bronze metallic beads, tapering with smaller beads at the corners and ends. Pay attention to stitch placement to achieve neat points.

2 *Outer line 1 (dark line)*

- Stitch a five-petal flower at the inner tip with dark colour 1 beads (3-cut) and metallic bronze centre.
- Couch line of beads following the outer design shape with dark colour 1 beads (3-cut).

3 Stitch lines of beads in dark turquoise joining the central shape to the scalloped shape A tapering with smaller beads as necessary.

4 *Outer line 2 (dark turquoise):*

Stitch outer line 2 next following the contour formed by Outer line 1 tapering with smaller beads at the points.

5 Fin-shaped section. Complete this section in ***right or left diagonal single layer technique*** as appropriate for each.

Each stitch has two bead colours and smaller beads are used to help taper where required. Create ***raised effect*** on the edge with ***outline padding*** in the manner described earlier in the analysis chart.

6 Complete the centre section:

a) Stitch the inner small five-petal flowers with dark colour and bronze centre.

b) Complete the shape using dark colour 2 beads tapering with smaller beads in the same colour as necessary.

c) Stitch fan shape:

i. Stitch a single bronze bead in the centre of each fan shape.

ii. Add single stitches with bugle beads creating the fan shape.

For longer lines add a small bead in the same colour on one or both ends as appropriate.

Do not add more than one bead at each end.

7 Add a crystal bead (topaz) in the centre and stitch surrounding the inner shape with transparent white AB beads and small clear turquoise beads.

Align with the shape/lines stitched previously using the ***line of held thread method***.

8 Stitch left and right diagonal lines of beads above the lines created at (3) using the same bead as that used for the fin-shaped section. Use the appropriate combination of bead size to create a harmonious flow.

9 Top of the central shape:

a) Add a single crystal bead (topaz) to the centre of the shape.

b) Stitch a semi-circle line using ***line of held thread method*** with transparent white AB beads.

c) Stitch single hexagon beads (dark metallic bronze) in a radiating shape over (b).

d) Complete the shape with the same beads as the fin-shaped section arranged in a fan shape.

For both (c) and (d) begin with a stitch in the centre, then stitch the right side and then the left.

SCROLLING SHAPE 3

1 Begin with the scalloped lines using ***couching technique 1–needle-koma method*** and bronze metallic beads, tapering with smaller beads at corners and ends. Pay attention to stitch placement to achieve nice points.

2 Stitch the focal point with a bronze centre encircled with transparent white AB beads using ***line of held thread-circle method.***

3 Stitch the radiating line above the centre circle with bronze beads using ***line of held thread–straight line technique.***

4 Stitch an elongated horse shoe shape abutting the centre circle with bronze beads tapering with smaller beads at the edge.

Finish this shape with a line of transparent white **AB** beads stitched with the ***line of held thread technique.***

5 Complete the shapes above the centre circle with stitches worked with ***separated single layer technique*** using two bead colours. Smaller beads are used to help taper where required.

All stitches should have space to lay flat.

6 Stitch round eight- petal flowers in the remaining scallop spaces.

7 Stitch the contour lines outside the shape using ***couching technique 1–combination needle koma method.***

The line on the left-hand side widens and the technique changes to ***diagonal single layer.***

Small scroll shape

1 Begin with the long line at the bottom of the shape which continues and follows the contour of shape 3.

Use ***couching technique 1–needle-koma method*** including the smaller rounder shapes at the end.

Taper with smaller beads.

2 Return to the beginning and work the other side.

3 Work the centre pattern above the cusp formed.

Begin with a single, small five-petal flower at the tip and join this to the cusp with the ***line of held thread- curved line technique.*** Add similar stitches of curved lines on either side of this central line.

4 Fit in radiating curved lines on both sides following the pattern with ***line of held thread-curved lines technique.***

5 Fill in the space between the lines with single stitches or 'v' shaped stitches (for larger patterns).

Note that lighter colours are being introduced for colour balance

---

Joining the shapes

1 Join shape 3 and the small scroll shape with a line of bronze beads and a second line of turquoise beads following the fabric design.

The upper brown line of the fabric is not stitched.

2 Stitch bugle beads along the lines indicated by the fabric design.

Add a small bead in the same colour if necessary to accommodate the space.

The remainder is left as negative space.

3 Above the turquoise line, work single stitches at an angle using silver beads.

These are interspersed with stitches of two or three beads as indicated by the fabric design.

4 Stitch the scalloped edge above these lines and add transparent white AB beads in each of the corners of the scallop.

5 Stitch the final outline with ***diagonal single layer technique*** using two bead colours.

These lines abut the single bead of (3) but otherwise maintain an even spacing with the scalloped edge. This adds interest to the design and better define the flow of the lines.

6 Complete the section by stitching small five or six-petal flowers as the space allows.

Turquoise beads are used to recede the flowers and the background is left as negative space to complement the adjoining sections.

Other small shapes

The 's' shapes above the line are stitched in a similar way so will not be detailed here save to say that the sequence in which they are stitched is based on the principles of foreground first and preservation of the shapes.

The background is stitched with the ***scatter effect technique*** using different colour beads matching the background fabric.

In some instances, where a clear light colour bead is used, a grey thread is used instead of white to recede the background further.

CENTRE STRIP

Central shape

1 Begin with a single bead encircled with a line of beads stitched in the ***line of held thread–circle method***.

2 Stitch the radiating single lines in ***line of held thread–straight line technique*** with bronze beads.

3 Work diagonal stitches using two bead colours with the ***separated single layer technique***.

Follow the inner contour lines of the shape. The two colours are similar to that used in the main strip and tie the two sections together.

4 Stitch another row of diagonal stitches in the ***separated single layer technique*** following the outer contour of the shape.

Leave the brown background exposed as negative space.

5 Place a straight stitch of two beads in a light colour between the tips of the shapes.

Arched shape

This area posed an interesting proposition The first instinct is to create lines following the contours which is an acceptable plan but a bit plain.

As this is a panel in its own right, I felt the desire to make it a bit special and went along with the plan to use colours and precision stitching to create a sunburst effect:

1 Stitching begins with the centre line.

2 Dark beads, a clear, light turquoise, an inside colour with turquoise outer and bronze beads are used.

3 The number and mix of beads are selected to create the sunburst effect and also the tapered bronze shape in the centre of the design.

4 The remainder of the shape is completed with ***scattere effect***.

Strip edges

Part A: Dark turquoise line

1 A line of single beads spaced and stitched in the direction of the line creates a thin edge.

Part B: Black Line

1 This line is the same width as the turquoise line but abuts an unpatterned band which will be filled with single stitches in ***scatter effect technique***.

2 To distinguish the two sections, diagonal stitches of two beads are worked.

Part C: Pattern between Part A and B

Here I have taken some artistic licence to not follow the fabric design, but to use it as guide:

1 A single bronze hexagon bead is stitched in the position of the brown triangle shapes.

2 Above this stitch, three converging stitches using silver beads are placed.

3 This is repeated for all the brown triangles in the fabric.

4 Between these shapes, a single bronze bead outlined by a semi-circle is stitched.

Around this semi-circle single bugle beads are stitched in a radiating pattern replicating the stitches of the central heart shape.

EDGING PATTERN OF MAIN STRIP

The edging is made up of several stripes but we shall ignore this fact and treat it as if each edge is made up of two lines, a black line on the inside and a turquoise line on the outside. The turquoise line that abuts the main stripe has already been stitched (see introduction after analysis section):

1 Stitch the turquoise line on the other side in the same manner.

2 Stitch the black lines with diagonal stitches of two beads oriented as a right diagonal.

After every stitch, use the same thread to tie down between the beads.

Patterned section:

1 Stitch the triangles by outlining each with two lines - bronze on the inside and the dark on the outer.

Work with ***line of held thread–straight line technique*** and pay attention to getting the point correct.

New sections are now formed.

2 Work a small five-petal flower in the mid-point of the section. Make sure that the bottom petal is lined up perpendicular to the base.

This should be the case for every section.

3 Stitch two bronze lines of five beads on each side of this small flower ending a bead space away from the petals.

4 Work six bugle beads arranged in a radiating manner above the small flower.

The outer limit of this pattern is aligned to the dark turquoise motif of the fabric.

5 On each side of (4) stitch five lines arranged in a sunburst pattern to complete the shape.

Two bead colours are used for each line and smaller beads are used to taper the lines:

a) The first stitch is a horizontal line at the base and it abuts the bronze line.

b) The second stitch is the second line from the top and it should abut the bugle bead at the edge and fit into the corner formed between the small flower and the bronze line.

c) Work the adjoining stitch to (b) working towards (a).

d) Fit in a stitch in the remaining space to complete the lower section.

e) Return to the top and work the last stitch which adjoins the remaining side of stitch (b).

f) Repeat for the remaining side.

6 All the other sections are stitched in a similar manner.

7 The final step is to work single and evenly spaced silver beads around the outer edges of the patterns in these sections.

They should end up as a continuous row of evenly spaced stitches undulating along the strip.

FINISHING

Random scatter effect technique is used to fill up any background spaces. Because of the patterns and the planned embroidery, there is not much background to be filled. The largest areas are the solid blue strips. These are filled with ***scatter effect technique–singles***.

For the other patterned area, use small beads in a clear colour matching as close to the background as possible to recede.

To summarise, both the case study designs, particularly Arabian Nights, are more complicated and challenging. This is rightly so as the projects in this book are geared towards developing skill in a structured manner. The latter projects do have some degree of challenge to them.

In the two case studies, the colours and design elements for Celebration of Flowers were followed as is without much deviation. For Arabian Nights, other colours were introduced to make the design work better for bead embroidery. Artistic licence was also used to make certain changes to design elements for the same reason. Design concepts that were discussed in the early part of the book were very much in play through the decision making process, so it is a good idea to become familiar with them.

ENJOY!!

1 Remove the beaded piece from the frame and cut out adding a 1cm (3/8") seam allowance.
2 Clip the corners if necessary.
3 Apply glue to the edge of the seam allowance only.
4 Fold the seam allowance under and glue the seam in position. The folded edge should lie just under the line of beads.
5 Fuse the interfacing or wadding to the wrong side of the lining piece.
6 Place the edges together and join with ladder stitch using a double thread for strength. The stitches should catch the fabric directly under the beads.
7 On completion fold or crumple tissue paper into shape and place inside. Steam gently. Remove the damp tissue and replace with dry tissue paper. Manipulate into shape and allow to dry overnight.

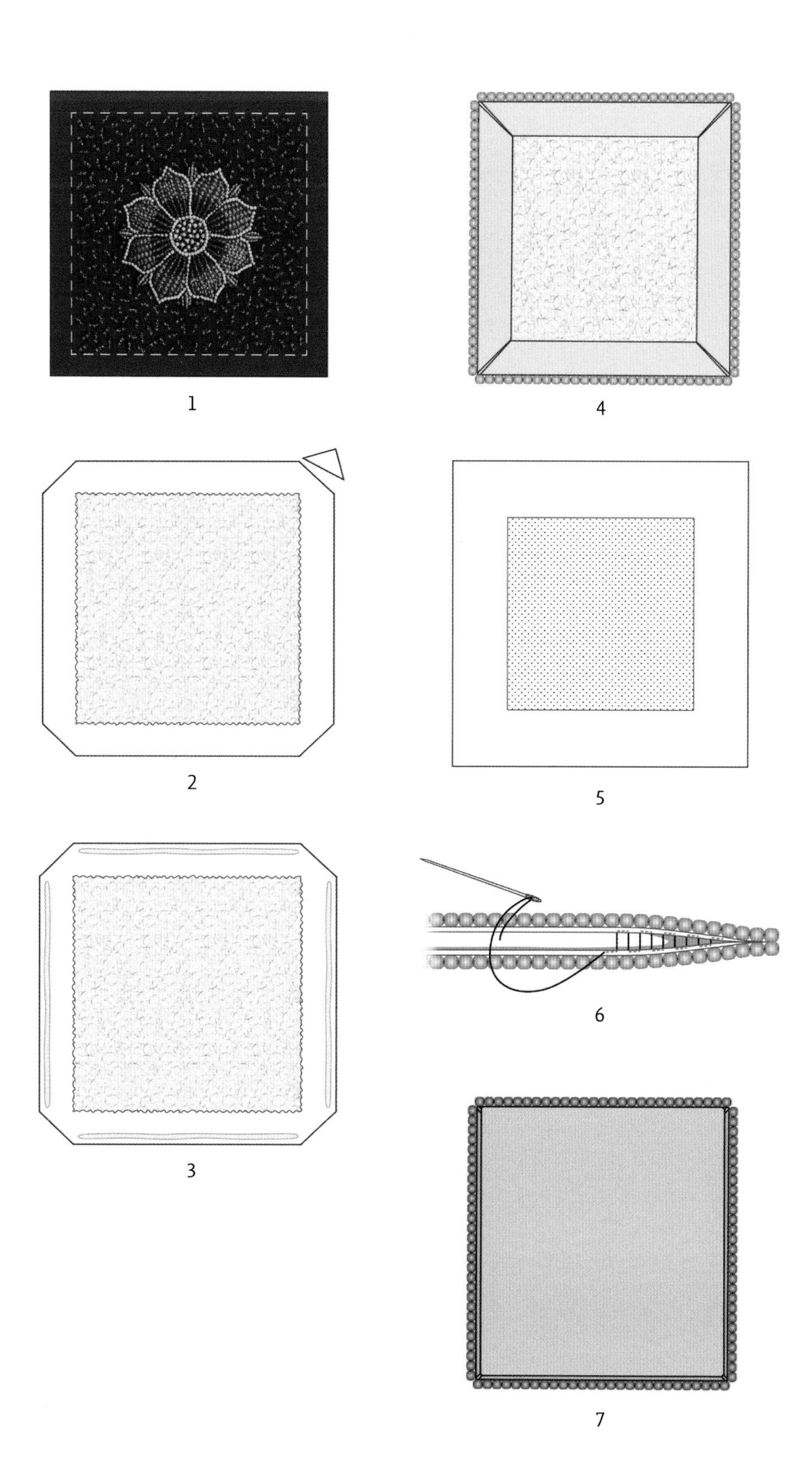

Author
Margaret Lee

Editor
Susan O'Connor

Assistant Editor
Ellaine Bronsert

Graphic Design
Lynton Grandison

Illustrations
Kathleen Barac

Photographic Styling
Fiona Fagan & Natalie Homan

Photography
Brendan Homan

Studio Management
Kristian & Andrea Fleming

Published in 2017 by
Inspirations Studios Corporation Pty Ltd
PO Box 10177
Adelaide Business Hub
South Australia 5000
Tel: +61 8 8293 8600
Email: info@inspirationsstudios.com
www.inspirationsstudios.com

The Art of Bead Embroidery–Japanese-Style
By Margaret Lee

An Inspirations Publication
ISBN 978-0-9923144-7-7

Printed & bound in China

INSPIRATIONS

For more of the world's most beautiful needlework publications, please visit our website:
www.inspirationsstudios.com

To discover more about Margaret Lee, her classes, touring schedules, and range of products, please visit her website:
www.magaretlee.com.au